Economics of oil and gas production

Economics of
Oil and Gas
Production

By

Roshdy Ebrahim, Ph.D

Copyright © 2018 Roshdy Ebrahim

All right reserved

ISBN: 9781980733591

Preface

Only when human societies started to utilize the fossil fuels, with their high levels of energy density, was the limit upon their size and complexity removed. The Renaissance and the resulting scientific revolution may have stretched that limit, but without the utilization of fossil fuels they could not have broken free. With fossil fuels, the change in the energy available was revolutionary, driving the rapid changes to human civilization over the past two centuries. The ratio of energy gained to energy spent for the fossil fuels was at least 80:1 for coal, 100:1 for oil, and 18:1 for natural gas. Also, the sheer volume of the energy that could be utilized dwarfed that which was previously available. Prior to this, the rate of energy use was limited by the depth and fertility of the soil, together with the vagaries of the weather. Now humanity had access to many millennia worth of photosynthesis which had been transformed into energy-dense substances and stored away under the ground. The only limitation was how quickly these new energy sources could be extracted. Naturally, the easiest ones went first. This huge increase in available energy has been the basis of modern industrial societies, which in turn have become addicted to this seemingly endless supply of cheap energy.

The year 1857 marked the beginning of commercial petroleum production in Rumania, followed in 1859 by the discovery of oil in Pennsylvania. Petroleum was found by the drillers under "Colonel" Drake, and crude refineries were soon built to separate the fractions. The most important fraction was kerosene, known as "illuminating oil", which rapidly became the dominant global fuel for lamps (replacing whale oil). In the early days, refinery output was about 50% kerosene, 10% gasoline, 10% lubricating oil, 10–15% fuel oil and the rest consisting of losses and miscellaneous by-products like tar.

Natural gas is currently the number three fossil fuel in terms of share of the global primary energy mix and for years the world has debated the potential for natural gas to play a critical part in building a more resilient and sustainable energy future. While the demand outlook is currently uncertain, advances in supply side technologies for unconventional resource development, led by advances in US shale gas operations, have changed the supply landscape and created new prospects for affordable and secure supplies of natural gas.

Oil and gas resources have provided much of the world's energy in the twentieth century and are expected to be an important part of the energy mix well into the twenty-first century. Currently, oil and gas provide approximately 63 % of primary energy consumption in Europe. However, energy security in the region remains a concern.

Contents

Preface 3
Contents 6
introduction 9
1. Production Phase 13
    1.1. The Stages of the Oil Production 15
    1.2. EXTRACTION PRINCIPLE 41
    1.3. EXTRACTION PROCESS 43
2. Crude oil production 53
    2.1. Global crude oil production 57
    2.2. Biological Upgrading of Heavy Crudes 61
    2.3. Offshore oil production 66
    2.4. Shale Oil 67
3. Gas production 74
    3.1. Gas production method 82
    3.2. Global natural gas production 83
    3.3. Natural Gas: EROI 10:1 and Declining; 23.7 % of Energy Usage 94
    3.4. Gas sales profiles; influence of contracts 97
    3.5. Shale gas production 102

- 3.5.1. Issues surrounding shale gas extraction 114
- 3.5.2. Global Perspective of Shale Gas Production 116
- 3.5.3. Optimization Models for Shale Gas Supply Chain 121
- 3.5.4. Shale Gas Supply Chain 124
4. Unconventional Oil and Gas 127
5. OPEC 134
   - 5.1. OPEC AND THE UNITED STATES 136
   - 5.2. OPEC Profits and Their Limit 144
6. World Petroleum Economics 147
   - 6.1. PETROLEUM INDUSTRY INVESTMENT 148
   - 6.2. Importance and Challenges of Petroleum 153
   - 6.3. Stages of Global Oil Development 157
   - 6.4. Colonial Concessions and the Cartelized Oil 158
   - 6.5. Decartelization of Oil and Competition 162
   - 6.6. SIZE AND RISK CONSIDERATIONS .. 165
   - 6.7. When Will Petroleum Run Out? 166
7. Oil and gas production in some countries . 172
   - 7.1. Oil and gas production in Nigeria .. 172

- 7.2. Oil and gas production in Egypt 180
- 7.3. Oil and gas production in Australia 190
- 7.4. Oil and gas production in china.....193
- 7.5. Oil and gas production in Russia ...200
- 7.6. Oil and gas production in Canada .208
- 7.7. Oil and gas production in USA.......217
- 7.8. Oil and gas Production in UK.........232

References 241

Biography of the author 246

introduction

In the mid-nineteenth century, mineral oil entered the market as an energy source. Refined oil in the form of petroleum and kerosene, for instance, rapidly gained a foothold in the lighting industry. At the time, oil deposits were much fewer in number than coal mines and were generally located in remote areas, at least from a Central European perspective. As a result, oil shipments began to significantly increase the volume of international trade. In the late nineteenth century, Western Europe imported its fossil oil mainly from the United States, and smaller amounts from Poland and Russia. Almost simultaneously, as the consumption of coal and crude oil increased sharply, several European countries such as France, Austria- Hungary, the Netherlands, Italy and Spain experienced industrial breakthroughs.

This period marked a major transition both in terms of economic structures and energy consumption patterns across Western Europe. In nineteenth-century Britain, the strong industrialization of the economy, the trend towards urbanization, and the growth of railway transportation sharply increased the consumption of coal, which became the principal energy source not only on the British Isles but also in various colonies. Coal remained the predominant energy source for decades until it was replaced by both petroleum and natural gas in the latter half of the twentieth century. Similar structural changes took place in the countries of other continents, such as the USA. [1]

Although the hydrocarbons produced from wells are usually listed as "oil" and "gas," there is an in-between product that sells for high prices. Hydrocarbons with three to five carbon atoms go under a bunch of names: gas condensate, natural gas liquids, drip gas, and "white gold." Some oil field workers pour the stuff directly into the gasoline tanks of their pickup trucks, a practice that is both dangerous and illegal.

Hydrocarbon chains are produced naturally by a wide assortment of plants and animals. Our ear wax is a mundane example. Hydrocarbons hate water; they do not mix with water; hydrocarbons repel water. Among chemists, "hydrophobic" is not a synonym for rabies.

---

[1] Marja Jarvela • Sirkku Juhola: Energy, Policy, and the Environment. Springer Science+Business Media, LLC 2011. P 33

Organisms, including people, are fundamentally bags of water. The best way of structuring a water-rich system is to use the contrast between water-hating (hydrophobic) components and water-loving (hydrophilic) entities. At one end of the scale, simple single-celled marine algae use hydrocarbon molecules to create a stable cell wall. At the other end, the myelin coatings that serve as electrical insulation around nerve cells in the human brain are also hydrocarbon chains.

The hydrocarbons made by organisms, from algae to humans, have a common oddity—literally an oddity: most of them contain an odd number of carbon atoms. [1]

Soaring oil prices, which surged to $147 a barrel in mid-2008, have drawn attention to the issue of supply and demand, suggesting that the present production capacity limits are being breached. It leads people to ask if we are running out of oil. The simple answer is: *Yes, we started doing that when we used the first gallon.* But the world is a long way from finally running out. What it does face, however, is the end of the *First Half of the Age of Oil*, which lasted 150

---

[1] K E N N E T H S . D E F F E Y E S: Hubbert's Peak. Princeton University Press. 2001. P 18: 19

years, giving rise to extraordinary changes in the way people lived.

The Planet supported some 300 million people at the time of Christ, 2,000 years ago, and the number barely doubled over the next seventeen centuries. Most people lived hand to-mouth rural lives. They were much dependent on local circumstances, facing famine if the harvest failed for climatic or other reasons. [1]

---

[1] C.J. Campbell: Campbell's Atlas of Oil and Gas Depletion. Colin J. Campbell and Alexander Wöstmann 2013. P 3

1. Production Phase

The production phase commences with the first commercial quantities of hydrocarbons (first oil) flowing through the wellhead. This marks the turning point from a cash flow point of view, since from now on cash is generated and can be used to pay back the prior investments or may be made available for new projects.

Minimizing the time between the start of an exploration campaign and 'first oil' is one of the most important goals in any new venture.

Development planning and production are usually based on the expected production profile which depends strongly on the mechanism providing the driving force in the reservoir. The production profile will determine the facilities required and the number and phasing of wells to be drilled. The production profile shown in the Figure is characterized by three phases: [1]

---

[1] Frank Jahn, Mark Cook and Mark Graham: HYDROCARBON EXPLORATION AND PRODUCTION. 2ND EDITION. Elsevier B.V. 2008. P 5

1. Build-up period During this period newly drilled producers are progressively brought on stream.

2. Plateau period Initially new wells may still be brought on stream but the older wells start to decline. Production facilities are running at full capacity, and a constant production rate is maintained. This period is typically 2–5 years for an oil field, but longer for a gas field.

3. Decline period During this final (and usually longest) period, all producers will exhibit declining production.

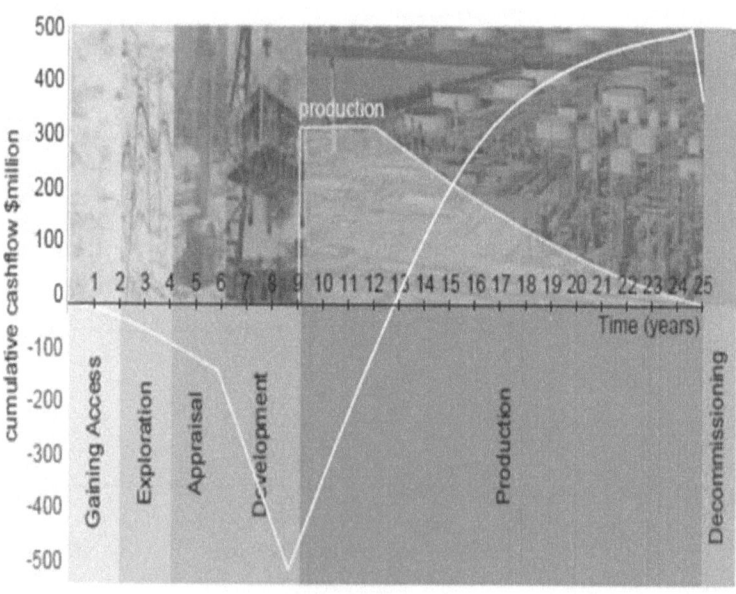

1.1. The Stages of the Oil Production

For our theoretical purpose, and from the perspective of the evolution of a modern industry, we divide the entire history of Middle Eastern oil into three stages of development: (1) the era of colonial oil concessions, 1901–50; (2) the era of transition and transformation, 1950–72; and (3) the era of postcartelization and globalization, since the mid-1970s. Given the early discovery of oil in the United States (1859), a slightly different, yet substantially overlapping, periodization may be applied to the US oil industry: (1) the era of classical cartelization and early oil trusts of 1870–1910; (2) the era of regulated neo-cartelization of 1911–72; and (3) the era of globalization, since 1974. These historical stages are not arbitrary but, as a corollary, reveal the evolution of capitalist social relations in the world oil industry.

A close examination of the entire period from 1870 to 1970 reveals that predominantly administered pricing (i.e., *unmediated* accounting calculations) and cartelized practices were the rule. Such a framework, however, had begun to lose its effectiveness in the 1950s and 1960s, as proliferating market forces did overcome the Achnacarry networks of the International

Petroleum Cartel (IPC) The 1928 Achnacarry Agreement inaugurated a new era of cartelization since the US antitrust law of 1911, which had led to the breaking up of Rockefeller's Standard Oil Trust. This was in response to the worldwide irreconcilable price wars that were in full swing at the time when there was no adequately developed global oil (capitalist) structure that would objectively mediate and manage all this perpetual chaos into a forcible, regulating reconciliation. This time, the control of oil meant cartelization of oil under the tutelage of a leviathan, from ocean to ocean, across the entire geography of the world, minus the Soviet territory. Blair charmingly summarizes the seven sacred tenets of this infamous agreement as follows:

Alarmed by the rapidity with which the price war has spread from India to America and then back to Europe, the heads of the three dominant international majors met at Achnacarry Castle in Scotland to prevent the recurrence of such disturbances. Walter C. Teague, then president of Exxon [Standard Oil of New Jersey], was quoted by a trade journal as saying, "Sir John Cadman, head of the Anglo-Persian Oil Co. [BP] and myself were guests of Sir Henri Deterding [head of the Royal Dutch-Shell] and Lady Deterding at Achnacarry for the grouse shooting, and while the game was a primary object of the visit, the problem of the

16

world's petroleum industry naturally came in for a great deal of discussion." Referred to generally as the As Is Agreement of 1928 or the Achnacarry Agreement, the product of this discussion was a document, dated September 17, 1928, setting forth a set of seven principles and outlining in general terms the policies and procedures to be followed in applying them. The principles provided for:

(1) accepting and maintaining as their share of markets the status quo of each member; (2) making existing facilities available to competitors on a favorable basis, but not at less than actual cost to the owner; (3) adding new facilities only as actually needed to supply increased requirements of consumers; (4) maintaining for each producing area the financial advantage of its geographical location; (5) drawing supplies from the nearest producing area; and (6) preventing any surplus production in a given geographical area from upsetting the price structure in any other area. The last point asserted that the observance of these principles would benefit not only the industry but consumers as well.

Given the necessity of tight control and awesome task of administration, the cartel had to issue several supplementary memoranda subsequent to the original agreement. Blair writes:

As the companies became increasingly familiar with the troublesome problems of trying to make a cartel operate successfully, the instructions had to cover a growing number of issues and at the same time become increasingly specific and precise. The principal topics with which they dealt were: (a) fixing quotas; (b) making adjustments for under- and overtrading; (c) fixing prices and other conditions of sale; and (d) *dealing with outsiders*.

The first stage in the development of the Middle Eastern oil industry coincided with the rudimentary development of capitalism and absence of full-fledged modern landed property. The private ownership of land excluded the ownership of subsoil, including the ownership of minerals underneath. A typical oil concession included the surrender of the right to explore, develop, and produce oil, natural gas, and related substances to the concessionaire, an international oil company. And from both legal and theoretical standpoints this surrender of the right to explore, develop, and produce should not be confused with the surrender of ownership of the resource (i.e., oil deposits in place) to the contracting oil companies.2 The term *concession*, rather than *lease*, refers to a contract between a private entity (i.e., a company) and a government (i.e., a would-be sovereign entity).

The oil concessions during this first stage (1901–50) had more or less the following commonalities:

1. They nearly covered the entire subsurface of the land in a country or territory.

2. They had a long duration that normally extended beyond 50 or 60 years.

3. They were only a handful of cartelized concessionaires worldwide.

4. The terms of the concessions were uniform.

5. The principal financial obligation was the uniform payment of royalty.

6. The financial terms were extremely moderate.

7. There was little change in the terms and conditions of these concessions.

The laws of the oil concessions [i.e., the colonial contracts] governing the *dominated* oil regions of the world, including the Middle East, are substantially different from the leasing contracts that prevail in the United States. It should be noted that the essential characteristic of the U.S. leasing practices stems from the structure of ownership of the subsoil, which is included as a part of the ownership of land.

Due to the observance of the *rule of capture,* in the United States, the materials obtained from the subsoil belong to the owner of the land.

Thus, from the beginning, capital investments in exploration, development, and production of oil had to come to terms with two separate systems of landed property in the subsurface across the globe. At the same time, from the standpoint of the stage of development, there emerged the tendency to a rudimentary valorization of landed property in these territories as opposed to a full-blown valorization in the United States (valorization of the landed property leads to the formation of rent, as a category, which in turn depends on the prior establishment of capitalism and capital as a social relation). That is why the industry as a whole—a disorderly conflation of different social relations in colonial and semi colonial settings—had to be managed by direct control and crude and unmediated cost and price calculations. Basing point accounting, which is illustrated in a bit of detail in the chapter on OPEC, was essentially the main springboard of pricing in the period.

The second stage in the development of the Middle Eastern oil industry was the gradual objectification of market forces that eventually led to decartelization and abandonment of administered pricing of oil through the crisis of 1973–74. This stage saw the uneasy coexistence of the declining cartelized mechanisms and practices, and the rising proliferation of market forces that carried and conveyed the spread of competition against the prearranged production, captive oil concessions, "gentleman's agreements," and arbitrary accounting of oil royalties (and rents) according to fictitious "posted" pricing.

Any transitional period, by necessity, tends to portray the amalgam of the vanishing past and the emerging future. The breakdown of the cartelization of oil was the consequence of certain evolutionary changes beyond the cartel's surrogate allocation and accounting system that had long been skillfully employed across the vast, untouched, and presumably passive geography of production. In one important sense, in contrast to its American counterpart, the history of the cartelization of international oil is a remarkable story of "primitive accumulation" (Thomson 1990). The cartelization of oil is indeed a prehistory of germinating capitalist social relations in these regions of the world—a prehistory of capital. Therefore, it would be a partial assessment if the focus of the analysis were to be merely on imperialism and outright plundering in this period. In addition to a more palpable issue of *nationalism*, the question of *class* that is often out of sight and lurking beneath all these occurrences must be taken to account in itself and as a prerequisite for organic unity of oil in globalization and thus the relevance of the *law of value* in the coming years. These two issues, although inseparable at the time, must be analytically dissected for the sake of the evolution of capitalism as an ultimate trump card and as a durable social relation, and the identity of imperialism as an unambiguous and identifiable period (i.e., a specific *epoch*) in the development of the former.

The transition in this second stage shows that the spread of capitalist social relations, via oil, was not only contradictory but also contagious.

Historically, however, the triumph of cartelization sowed the seeds of its own destruction. Introduction of foreign capital in the exploration, development, and production of oil and the germinating capitalist social relations in many of these oil territories have eventually led to the valorization of landed property under capitalism. Therefore, this transitional stage is the beginning of the unraveling and dismantling of the ad hoc and fragmented accounting schemes that stitched the US oil basing-point system, at the Gulf of Mexico, to the newly devised (i.e., the cut-rate) posted prices at the Persian Gulf. This provided the companies with an opportunity to pocket not only the monopoly oil profits but also the lion's share of the oil royalties.

As we have expressed elsewhere in this book, some of the basic identifying features of this period are (1) the arbitrary division of oil profits and oil rents—starting with 50–50 profit sharing, (2) the elimination of "phantom freight" and the designation of a second basing point at the Persian Gulf,3 (3) the nationalization (1951) and subsequent denationalization (1954) of oil in Iran, (4) the formation of the Organization of Petroleum Exporting Countries (OPEC), and (5) the rise of independent oil companies and the demise of the Achnacarry.

During this period, given the desire for stabilizing the basing-point price of oil at the Gulf of Mexico, US domestic oil has also been controlled (Blair 1976: 121–203). This basing-point system, erected upon the wellhead price of US oil (at the Gulf of Mexico), was used as a universal (accounting) yardstick for the pricing of oil anywhere in the world (Federal Trade Commission 1952).

The so-called 50–50 profit-sharing was not really about sharing the oil profits equally between the oil exporting state and the IPC.

This scheme was motivated by the dissatisfaction over the 1943 IPCsanctioned oil laws that were ratified by the government of President Isaұas Medina Angarita in Venezuela. These laws had given carte blache to a consortium of oil companies that either operated as the springboard of the IPC in Latin America or capitulated to the same cause. However, the Medina government imposed higher taxes on profits by foreign capital and manipulated the 1944 Venezuelan national budget in such a way as to show earnings equivalent to 50 percent of oil company profits. This raised eyebrows in the US State Department that was at the time behaving more zealous and acting "more catholic than Pope" in such matters. But the IPC was more relaxed and thought that as long as there was no violation against the 1943 laws, this measly (income) tax would be tolerable. The confidence of the IPC was not built on toleration alone, but on the solidrock foundation of fabulous oil acquisitions and lucrative earnings, which were kept out of sight and guarded meticulously in an off-thebook fashion, and which would offset tens of thousands of times such nickel-and-dime propositions.

After the left-of-center government of Rmula Batancout took over and J. P. Pérez Alfonso was at the helm in all oil-related issues, eventually on November 12, 1948, and not without a fair amount of uphill battle and struggle, Venezuela was able to pass a new income tax law that forged "a 50 percent rate on any sum by which the company's net profits exceeded the government's share of the company's earnings".

A careful look at this "sharing" scheme, of course, would reveal that this is not a genuine 50–50 sharing of the profits, but a simple division of "earnings" that were formally kept on the books, "net" of tangible, intangible costs from exploration, drilling, pipelines to refinery runs, intracompany and intercompany transfers, discretionary costs attributed to the administration, and finally countless other categories of real or fabricated costs—all wonderfully hidden by design from the purview of oil exporting governments.

Therefore, a more fitting description for this arrangement would a 50–50 window dressing. But there is no question that this was a better deal than the arrangement based on fixed royalty.

Venezuela's struggle under Alfonso toward "50–50 profit sharing," had also borne fruit in Saudi Arabia in 1950. Yet, in Iran, due to characteristic intransigence displayed by both the British government and the Anglo-Iranian Oil Company (AIOC), even subsequent to the nationalization of oil and the ensuing negotiations, there was neither enough wisdom on the part of the British nor adequate maturity on the part of the AIOC that the world they had been used to had already changed even within the IPC. In this period, the dogmatic attitude of the British government and archaic conduct of the AIOC as a government within the government in Iran is a shameful reminder that little had changed in Britain with regard to the postwar international polity. The following passage captures the disagreement between Britain and the United States on the question of 50–50 profit sharing for Iran:

At a luncheon meeting [of early April 1951 in London] characterized by "tenseness" and "sparring comments," McGhee [U.S. Assistant Secretary of State] tried to persuade Fraser [Chairman of the Board of the AIOC] to consider current realities in Iran and be more forthcoming.

Fraser was adamant, saying that McGhee's understanding of the situation was wrong and that there was no need to give Iran any concessions. "Fifty-fifty is a fine slogan, but it seems to be of dubious practicality," Fraser added. McGhee concluded that Fraser "had not yet learned."

As documented rather judiciously and with exceptional precision by Elm (1992), the rumored offer of 50–50 profit-sharing to Iran by the British government or by the AIOC was not an offer at all;

Britain wanted nothing short of restoring the 1933 oil concession and reinstating the AIOC to its prenationalization status (Elwell-Sutton, 1955).5 That is why a violent removal from office of an elected prime minster, who enjoyed unprecedented international support, in a sovereign nation was the only option. Mohammad Mossadegh (1882–1967) was finally toppled in a violent CIA coup d'état in August 19, 1953, in Iran. A faint twinkle of colonial victory shone in Winston Churchill's cunning eyes. The tyranny of the containment of genuine nationalism (and messy democracy) though was the hang-up of his American counterparts (see Kinzer 2003). Hanging on by the thin thread of the Soviet threat (and catalyst of Cold War) was merely an afterthought of this badly choreographed tragedy. John Foster Dulles (secretary of the state) and his brother Allen Dulles (director of CIA) in the Eisenhower administration, who had a heavy hand in minute details, would chuckle at all this nonsense and at the naiveté and sophomoric reconstruction of the facts by historians (and by international relations specialists) who have long been perpetuating this myth. Those who have made a cottage industry of the Soviet threat and Mossadegh's removal may not have a clear idea about the art of theorization and distinction of *core* from *catalyst* in formulation of theory. These scholars discounted the very fact that the 1951 nationalization of oil in Iran was a threat to the survival of the IPC and that the question at that *stage* was oil—and oil only. Our thesis acquires further solidity with the events, including US reaction, surrounding the formation of OPEC in 1960. It is instructive to know that the legacy of Mossadegh's nationalization did not expire with American (and British) coup d'état against his government. Mossadegh's gift of self-determination was received rather enthusiastically by the watchful eye of the world while he was in internment under the control and custody of the Shah's regime, on behest of the US government. In 1955, after a long debate, the Third Committee (known as the committee of 60) of the UN General Assembly adopted a resolution that supported the right of economic and political self-determination— including freedom of disposal of one's own national wealth and resources. The only three members opposed to this resolution were representatives from Britain, the United States, and the Netherlands.

The 1955 text adopted by the UN General Assembly reads:

1. All peoples have the right of self-determination. By virtue of this right they freely determine their political status and freely pursue their economic, social and cultural development.

2. The peoples may, for their own ends, freely dispose of their natural wealth and resources without prejudice to any obligations arising out of international economic cooperation, based upon the principle of mutual benefit, and international law. In no case may a people be deprived of its own means of subsistence.

3. The states, parties to the covenant having responsibility for the administration of Non-Self-Governing and Trust Territories shall promote the realization of the right of self-determination in such Territories in conformity with the provisions of the United Nations Charter. (UN Doc. A/C.3/L.489 in Hyde 1956: 856) Returning to the run-up to the formation of OPEC, as the new and bountiful discoveries of cheaper oil in the Persian Gulf region came to a fruition, the new oil had not only displaced the US markets to the west of Suez but continued also on the way to markets on the US eastern seaboard. Thus, the regional oil markets adjacent to the Western Hemisphere were supplied with the oil from the Persian Gulf. This prompted the international oil cartel to cut the Persian Gulf posted prices to prevent the interregional flow of oil toward the US market, thus complying with the tenet of the 1928 "As Is Agreement" reached in the Achnacarry. Historically, the posted price at both Gulfs functioned as an allocating mechanism for transferring and disbursing crude within the worldwide networks of the cartel.

Therefore, while cutting the Persian Gulf posted price reduced the flow of oil from this region, it also diminished the oil royalties for this region both in terms of the magnitude (per barrel) and the quantity of output.

As explained elsewhere in this volume, the founding of OPEC was a response to the continuous cuts in the posted prices by the IPC in the late 1950s. The posted price of oil was cut due to a combination of factors, such as the 1958 recession, expansion of Russian oil production, and the imposition of the 1959 oil import quota on the US domestic oil market, which was by far the largest in the world.

The last factor, which was devised to discourage competition from the US independent producers, is indeed the tip of the iceberg of US government endorsement of As Is Agreement (the Achnacarry) at the expense of both the US domestic consumers and the royalty earners of the Persian Gulf oil region. This was, however, concealed by the US government under the convenient cloak of "national security."

It is noteworthy to point out in passing that once the deception of national security—and the pretense of "strategic oil"— was concocted, the tensions between the Anti-Trust Division of the US Justice Department and the State Department over the violation of the Sherman Anti-Trust Act of 1890 and the pertinent antitrust law of 1911 subsided once and for all. This ingenious invention is only the tip of the blunder associated with the myopic, immature, and intransigent foreign policy of this period. The mood against the founding of OPEC in the Western media can be captured in the following passage:

After ten days of relative silence [. . . the Anglo-American] press began to attack OPEC openly. The *New York Times* mentioned the organization for the first time on 25 September 1960 and then only to call it an "international cartel". Expressing the feelings of the oil companies, the paper stated "[g]enerally, the oil companies are opposed to any such government cartel. They consider it impossible to establish a fair and workable program (of regulated production) and fear that the result, in the long term, would be withering away of market outlets."

. . . The threat was clear. A few days later the paper returned to the subject, accusing OPEC of "an interference with the principle of free enterprise" and stating that "oil men here do not believe that the international oil organization formed in Baghdad provides the answer to the problem of stabilizing prices."

Behind the scenes and in concert and choreographed with the media, the unofficial US foreign policy was the policy of status quo in line and indeed hand-in-glove with the basic tenets of the Achnacarry.

This, for instance, can be seen from the US defensive attitude in failing to recognize OPEC for nearly a half a decade after its formation.

The following passage from the 1964 US-UK Memorandum of Conversation, while shedding light on the role of the US State Department, also reveals the early idea of the countervailing "oil consumer grouping" against OPEC, long before the 1970s:

We envisage, said Sir Geoffrey [Harrison, Britain's Deputy Foreign Secretary], that a confrontation on OPEC issues might take place in different ways. (1) We might find ourselves in a position . . . to support the companies. This would have many drawbacks, including the invoking of Arab nationalist sentiments [that] provide potential for Soviet meddling and create internal political difficulties in the countries concerned. Because of these fears, the Shah [of Iran] was prepared to get out in front in order avoiding [*sic*] enactment of sanctions at the [24 December 1963] Riyadh OPEC meeting. He, in fact, blocked sanctions against companies. (2) A confrontation might arise with the Western European consuming governments . . . if difficulties over OPEC should lead to an interruption in the supply . . . (3) A price rise could likewise provoke a Western European consumer combination to oppose OPEC. However, we incline to the belief that a rise in prices will come about in any event and the European governments will just have to learn to live with it . . . Mr. Kelly [U.S. Assistant Secretary of the Interior for Mineral Resources] expressed agreement in principle with everything Sir Geoffrey had said . . . We are also worried about a consumer/producer confrontation and there is a chance we might provoke this sooner than necessary . . . By focusing European attention now on Middle East oil problems, we may stimulate European thinking on an oil consumer grouping to counter OPEC . . . *We wish to avoid a confrontation between OPEC and OECD* in 1964 . . . Sir Geoffrey said he wished to reaffirm the joint position reached in the June [1963] talks on the desirability of maintaining a stance of neutrality and nonrecognition of OPEC.

Britain's inflated posturing and American naiveté toward OPEC turned out to be a flop. It took nearly six years for the US government to realize that it was virtually alone in nonrecognition of OPEC. Thus, the belated US action by default:

The U.S.-U.K. policy of neutrality and non-commitment towards OPEC detailed in CA-386 (paragraph 8) has not prevented the OPEC from obtaining recognition from international organizations, specifically the ECOSOC and UNCTAD, and Austria has granted diplomatic status to the organization and its personnel. *In light of these and other successes by the OPEC, the U.S. [government] intends to review* the present policy towards the OPEC and consider if some other policy towards the organization might more usefully serve U.S. interests.

Toward the end of the 1960s, there occurred, inter alia, three major developments that entirely undermined the cartelized character of the industry in favor of the rising objective market forces and spot oil prices globally. First, there appeared transformative macroeconomic changes in OPEC's relationship with the IPC; this was reflective of changes in the internal development and potential integration of the oil exporting countries into the world economy. Second, there emerged the proliferation of independent oil companies, which is a telling story about the internal turmoil and erosion of power in the cartelized system of Achnacarry (1928–72). This was a grand experiment on the so-called barriers to entry, and in retrospect it was settled unilaterally by the eventual collapse of the IPC in 1972. To identify some of these

35

"independents," names such as Ashland Oil, Occidental Petroleum, Amerada Hess, Marathon Oil, Continental Oil, City Service, Sun Oil, Union Oil, Philips Petroleum, and Getty Oil come to mind (see Blair 1976, Bina 2012c). Finally, there was a considerable increase in the exploration and development costs of US domestic oil, the costliest in the world, in both per/barrel and absolute magnitude.

The latter, in turn, translated into a significant increase in the cost of US domestic oil production. At this time, a close inspection of the US oil fields revealed (1) considerable fragmentation of the new oil leases associated with the US domestic exploration activities, (2) sizable fragmentation of oil leases (i.e., the dispersion of royalty ownership) in the producing oil fields in need of unitization and application of advanced oil recovery, (3) the veritable decline of the US oil finding rate (oil reserves added per well), following the 1970 US production peak, and (4) significant increase in the cost of successive capital investments in the secondary and tertiary recoveries in the aged US oil fields.

In the meantime, in the early 1970s, the Texas Railroad Commission abandoned the policy of market demand prorationing after nearly four decades since the discovery of bountiful East Texas field.

As Blair (1976) articulates, the 1932 prorationing (or, as labeled rather artfully, "conservation") of Texas oil rights after the Achnacarry Agreement was a substitute for unitization of the fields (and the application of advanced recovery), which practically led to the destruction of billions of barrels of ultimate US oil recovery. On January 1, 1970, the US federal oil depletion allowance was reduced from 27.5 to 22.0 percent. On August 15, 1971, the Nixon administration instituted the first phase of price controls. On January 11, 1973, mandatory price control turned into voluntary control. On August 17, 1973, the Nixon administration imposed a two-tier price ceiling on domestic oil: old oil (produced at or below 1972 levels from existing wells) was to be sold at March 1973 prices plus 35 cents; new oil (produced above 1972 levels from existing wells and from new wells) was free of control. In 1972 the infamous 1959 oil import quota (a friendly gesture to the IPC in the name of "national security") was rescinded (Blair 1976: 152–86). This is the same program that triggered further cuts in the Persian Gulf posted prices and led to the formation of OPEC.

Finally, there was the devaluation of the US dollar, first in December 1971 and subsequently in February 1973, respectively at 8.5 and 10 percent. All these developments transpired well before the October 16, 1973, and January 1, 1974, OPEC price hikes. On November 15, 1974, the International Energy Agency (IEA) was formed.

Eventually, the grand cartelized network of Achnacarry was unraveled piece by piece during the transition period. The gentleman's agreement gave way to the tumultuous forces of the market. The lack of control over the increasing volume of oil outside of the cartel's network did the trick. The development of adequate capitalist structure in the oil exporting countries led to de facto valorization of landed property in oil. This in turn transformed the nature of OPEC, notwithstanding the Trojan horses of the golden years of Pax Americana within OPEC that desperately searched for a middle ground. The US domestic oil fields were rationalized; the global oil industry was reorganized and unified through the crisis; and the price of production of the US oil had become the regulating price of production for the entire industry worldwide. The world oil entered into the era of globalization with unified market prices, global differential oil rents, and plenty of volatility.

38

The 1973–74 crisis must be considered as the mirror of much larger manifold transformations, namely (1) the worldwide unification of the oil industry—from the lowest to the highest cost structure— under one pricing rule, (2) the de facto nationalization and concurrent transnationalization of oil against the IPC by the oil rentier states, (3) the decartelization of US oil and rationalization of the US oil industry, (4) the universal valorization of the landed property and competitive formation of global differential oil rents, (5) the transformation of OPEC from a rudimentary rent setter to a full-fledged rent collector, (6) the proliferation of global oil markets, abolition of posted prices, and formation of global oil spot (and futures) prices, and (7) the redundancy of the unmediated (physical) access, utopian self-sufficiency, and dependency on a particular oil region.

The era of cheap oil/expensive oil was over. The law of one price (underpinned by *regulating capital* in the US domestic oil) had become a universal rule for all oil across the board. Yet, in realpolitik, the deception of national security, via the allegation of dependency and demand for access, led to tough talks and threats against Pax Americana's favorite son, the Shah of Iran, by Henry Kissinger and to the panic plan of a Rapid

Deployment Force by the Carter administration.7 On the supposedly analytic front, the post-1970s geopolitics of oil had essentially centered on the traditionally fragmented quarrels over the de-Americanization8 of oil and concern over US domestic oil production, consumption, and imports. And it took nearly another decade for the United States, OPEC, and the emerging world to realize that ultimately these epochal changes were irreversible.

Decartelization of oil also cut the umbilical cord of the US foreign policy from oil. The IPC was in a variety of ways a beachhead with multiple economic and political outposts in the oil-producing countries. The companies within the IPC often operated as a government within a government in many of these countries. The Anglo- Iranian Oil Company in Iran was a notorious class by itself in this regard. This was probably as important, if not more, as the economic aspect of oil, particularly for the United States. [1]

---

[1]Cyrus Bina: A Prelude to the Foundation of Political Economy. PALGRAVE MACMILLAN. 2013. P 100:112

1.2. EXTRACTION PRINCIPLE

If two liquids, a solvent and a solute, are in a homogeneous solution and a third liquid is introduced into the solution, there will be two liquid layers separated into two homogeneous solutions as shown in Figure 10.1. This type of phenomenon will occur only for certain selected third liquids, which solubilise any one or both of the components, which were formerly in the homogeneous solution. Phase separation occurs due to the difference in density of the resulting solutions. This phenomenon is utilized for separating two miscible liquid components from a solution and such a method is called extraction. If the solute (A), the carrier liquid (B) in the feed mixture, and the pure solvent (C) are brought in intimate contact by thorough mixing, the solute will transfer to the solvent due to the concentration gradient set up between the feed and the solvent. This transfer (mass transfer) process will continue until the equilibrium concentration of the solute between the feed and the solvent is achieved, as long as the feed and the solvent are in intimate contact.

Extraction is applicable for separating components that are difficult to separate by distillation, settling, or other means. For instance, if the boiling points of the components are very close or the desired components are too sensitive to high temperature,

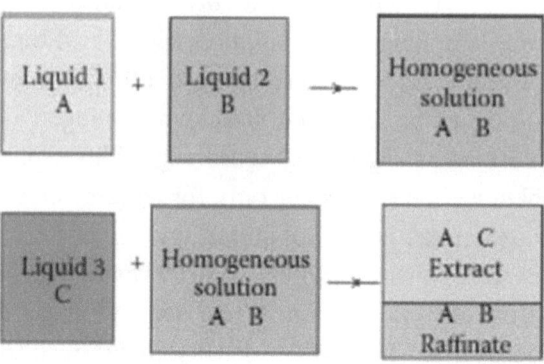

when "C" is not soluble in "B"

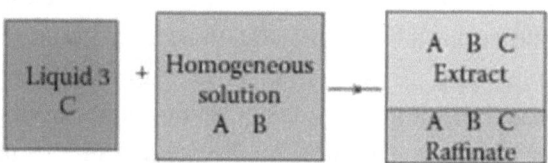

when "C" and "B" are also partially soluble

extraction should be used as the best method for separation. When all the components involved in extraction are in liquid phases, the process is known as liquid extraction.

While the feed is a solid mixture containing the solute, extraction by a liquid solvent is carried out and the process is known as leaching. For example, separation of aromatic hydrocarbons from vacuum distillates by furfural (solvent) is an example of liquid extraction, whereas removal of paraffinic hydrocarbons from waxy distillates by ketone (solvent) is an example of leaching. In refineries and petrochemical plants, extraction processes also involve more than one solute and more than one solvent. [1]

1.3. EXTRACTION PROCESS

Any extraction process requires three operating steps, i.e., mixing, separating, and solvent recovery. The solvent and the feed must be mixed intimately to transfer the solute to the solvent. After mixing, the final mixture is allowed to settle, while two phases containing the solvent rich phase or the extract and the solvent lean phase or raffinate are separated. These phases will separate by gravity or by centrifuge settler. Usually, the solvent is also partially soluble in the feed and vice versa and as a result both the extract and raffinate phases will contain solvent, solute, and the carrier components. The next step will be to recover the solvent from these phases usually by distillation. Finally, the extract phase will yield solute and

---

[1] Uttam Ray Chaudhuri: Fundamentals of Petroleum and Petrochemical Engineering. Taylor and Francis Group. 2011. P 235: 236

the raffinate phase will be the feed liquids nearly free from solutes. The success of any extraction process depends on various factors as listed below. The steps for an extraction process are schematically explained in Figure 10.2. [1]

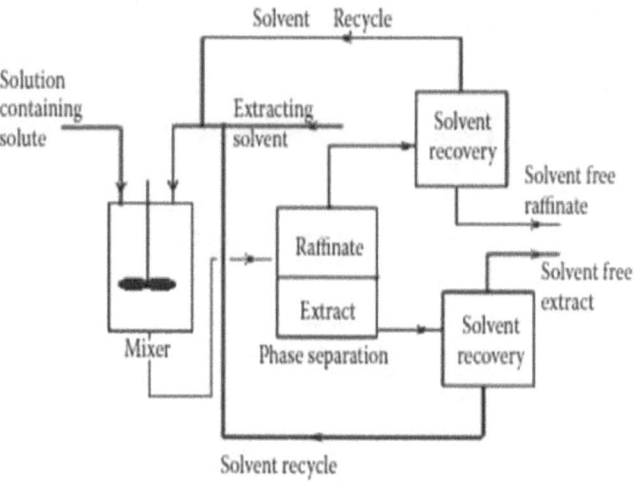

The *gas lift* method employs high pressure gas, usually air or carbon dioxide, which is introduced into the well through the annulus and oil is carried through the inner tubing, leading to the well-head piping. Initially, the well is filled with the mud fluid and the oil cannot move up owing to the hydrostatic head of

[1]Uttam Ray Chaudhuri: Fundamentals of Petroleum and Petrochemical Engineering. Taylor and Francis Group. 2011. P 236

the mud fluid. As the gas enters the annulus and piping, the density of the mud column decreases and the hydrostatic head decreases, and as a result, the mud fluid is lifted by the oil pressure.

A mud–oil mixture is collected and separated on the surface tanks. When complete displacement of mud takes place from the well and from the pores of the layer near

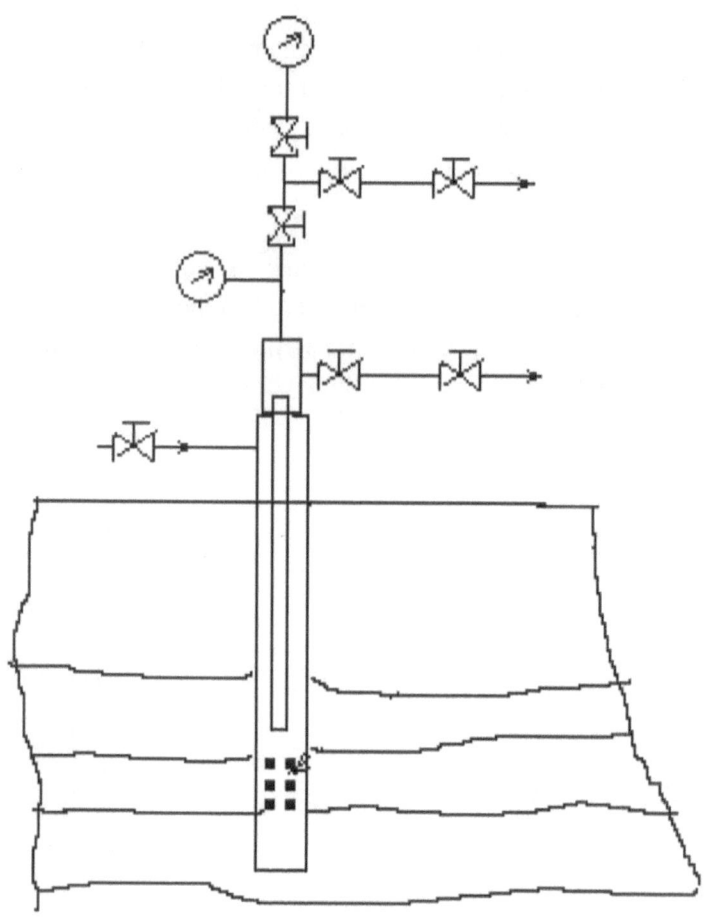

the borehole by the oil pressure, oil production starts increasing. Such a schematic gas lift operation is shown in Figure 1.13.

A *sucker rod lift* well contains a piston (or a plunger) pump lowered into the inner tubing. The piston is operated by a metallic wire or rod leading through the tubing and above the well head and connected to a wire rope from a hanger attached with a reciprocating driving system at the base of the well head. The piston is contained in a cylinder with non-return valves fitted at both ends. During the upstroke of the piston, the bottom valve opens, keeping the top valve closed and, as a result, the cylinder pressure falls below the reservoir pressure, forcing oil to enter the cylinder. While during the down stroke of the piston, the upper valve opens and the bottom valve closes and oil in the cylinder is pushed up to the tubing through the upper valve. Thus, the volume of oil displaced upward in the tubing is proportional to the stroke length of the piston. When the tubing is filled with oil after repeating the reciprocating operation, oil starts flowing upward and is collected. A schematic sucker rod lift arrangement is shown in the Figure. A *submersible pump well* contains a centrifugal or screw pump installed in the tubing lowered into the borehole. Both the electric motor and the pump are submersed in the well bottom. Electric cable sealed in a flameproof arrangement is lowered into the well hole through the tubing. The motor is usually kept below the pump in the tubing. Pumps are small in diameter (3–6 in), multistage centrifugal or screw pumps. Since entrainment of sand particles and gas may cause problems to the centrifugal pumps, modern wells are using high capacity multistage screw pumps that can carry slurries, viscous oil, and even gas.

In fact, future wells will deliver more viscous oil contaminated with sand and clay materials, therefore, increasing use of submersible screw pumps will take place in modern and existing wells. Modern screw pumps with a diameter as small as 6 in with a capacity of 100 m^3 or more per day and with a head of 1000 m are being used

Economics of oil and gas production

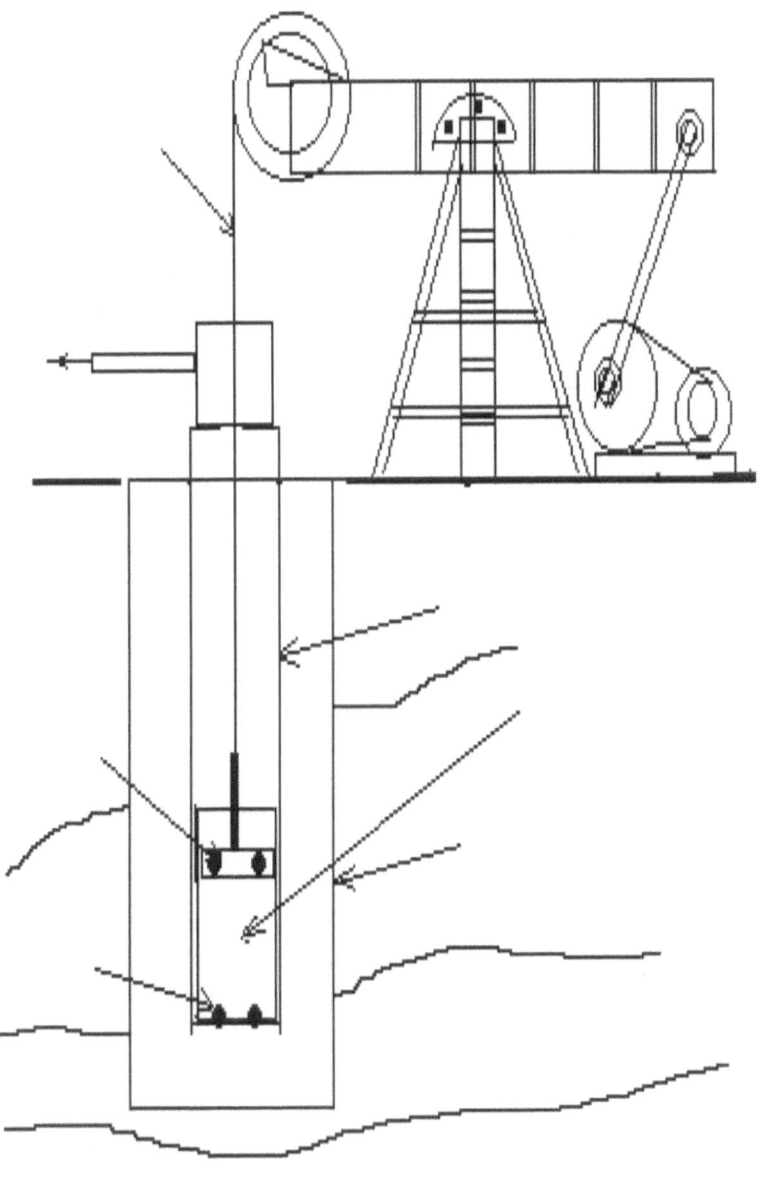

in wells. The number of stages of a pump may be more than 100 tightly fitted in a tubing. A submersible pumping well is shown in the Figure.

The *hydraulic pumping* method employs a special type of tubing that consists of two tubes. The inner tube is of a larger diameter in which the plunger or the diaphragm pump is lowered into the borehole. The plunger or the rod of the diaphragm is forced by pumping a liquid over it in a reciprocating manner. Oil is discharged through the outer pipe through its annular space and is delivered to the surface tank. This method does not require lowering any electrical cable and no wire for actuating the plunger.

A high-pressure reciprocating surface pump delivers the liquid forced up and down the plunger of the pump in the borehole in a reciprocating manner. The plunger pump can be withdrawn on the surface from the inner pipe by forcing liquid through the annular outer pipe. Such a pumping arrangement is shown in the Figure. The rate of production from a single well may not be large. Hence, a good number of wells, varying from 100 to 1,000 wells depending on the rate of production, are drilled in the area where the formation is spread. Excitation (stimulation) of the wells by gas or water injection from the surrounding injection wells (judiciously located) is extremely necessary to increase reservoir pressure to the flowing wells. Modern methods also employ combustion of oil in the surrounding wells to push the oil in the formation by heat effect on reducing viscosity in the porous channels of the formation. A proper temperature gradient is essential from the channels of the combustion zone to the target well. Crude oil from all these wells are collectively routed to storage and conditioning. [1]

---

[1] Uttam Ray Chaudhuri: Fundamentals of Petroleum and Petrochemical Engineering. Taylor and Francis Group. 2011. P 16: 20

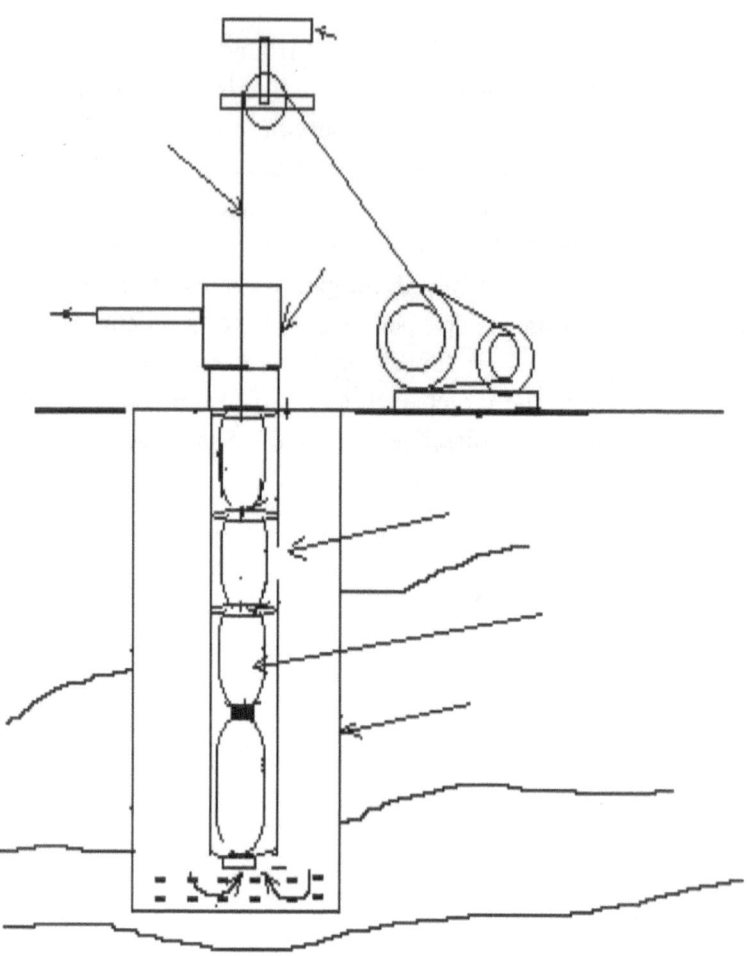

2. Crude oil production

According to secondary sources, OPEC crude oil production averaged 30.07 mb/d in 2014, a decrease of 0.16 mb/d over the previous year. It was higher in 2H14 by 0.45 mb/d to average 30.30 mb/d compared with 1H14. OPEC's share of the global crude oil supply in 2014 dropped to 32.6 per cent (–0.16 mb/d) from 33.5 per cent the previous year. The main reduction came from Libya, while the greatest increase was seen in Iraq, according to secondary sources. Moreover, OPEC crude oil production was seen lower by 0.91 mb/d to average 30.68 mb/d in 2014, compared with a year earlier, based on direct communication. [1]

Since 2005, oil production has been running, on average, around 74 million barrels per day, with new production flows only just offsetting the depletion and reduced flows from current wells. At some point, which may be very near, the relatively small flows from the new production fields will not be able to offset the decline of the older much more generous fields, and the daily flow of oil will start to decline. Global oil production has become much like Lewis Carroll's Red Queen, running faster just

---

[1] Organization of the Petroleum Exporting Countries. Annual Report 2014. P 19

to stay in the same place. Even now, the current production plateau may be masking a decline in the net energy provided from oil production, as increases in oil volumes from tar sands, deep water, and shale just balance the depletion of higher net energy conventional oil fields. We may be getting the barrels, but we are not getting the same amount of net energy they used to deliver. Shale oil has been touted as a huge new source of energy, facilitating "energy independence" for the USA. It has allowed the US oil production to increase, but at the global level, has only aided in offsetting the depletion of current wells. The long-term viability of shale oil production has been questioned given the relatively low per well production and very high depletion rates. Some researchers have also pointed to the relatively small "sweet spots" within shale oil areas, with well productivity falling off rapidly with an increase in the distance from the sweet spot. [1]

As oil-exporting nations increase in population and become wealthier, domestic demand for oil grows and the balance left for export falls. Adding to the problem, there is a tendency for such nations to keep energy costs low to either support the local economy or buttress unelected elites, as in many of the

---

[1] Roger Boyd: Energy and the Financial System Springer Cham Heidelberg New York Dordrecht London 2013. P 31

Middle East countries. This only increases the amount of their energy production used domestically, as low prices foster demand and inefficient usage. Thus, the peak of "internationally available oil" will happen sooner than the global production peak. The fall from that peak may be accelerated as the oil exporters may decide to reduce production of their scarce and increasingly valuable oil resources to stretch out the period of required transition. Already, Indonesia and Egypt have moved from being oil exporters to oil importers and Mexico, Malaysia, and Iran are seeing oil exports fall faster than their overall production levels. This is not good news for countries that rely heavily on oil imports like the USA, China, Japan, and Europe. [1]

To make things even worse, an increasing amount of world oil exports are coming from countries which are less stable than the more established suppliers. Some very interesting countries have been added to the list of significant oil exporters, such as Nigeria, Angola, and Algeria. When you think of these three countries what kind of images come to mind—images of peace, lawfulness, honesty and happiness? Or do images of scary people with guns, civil wars, political activists being

---

[1] Roger Boyd: Energy and the Financial System Springer Cham Heidelberg New York Dordrecht London 2013. P 32

executed, or widespread graft and outright theft by the powerful come to mind? Nigeria, with a production of over 2 million barrels per day, is now the eighth biggest oil exporter in the world compared with places like the USA and Europe. Close behind in oil production volume is the country of Angola. Older readers may remember the initials MPLA (Movement for the Liberation of Angola), FNLA (National Front for the Liberation of Angola), and UNITA (National Union for the Total Independence of Angola), three groups that fought a very nasty civil war in Angola over nearly three decades. Not far behind is Algeria, which only lifted a state of emergency in 2011 and where security is so lacking that at the beginning of 2013 a natural gas facility was attacked and several foreign workers killed. Another problematic country is Libya, where a stable dictatorship has been replaced by tribal warfare and ongoing disruptions to oil exports. So, if the inhabitants of the oil-exporting countries are not consuming more of their oil themselves, their exports may be affected by some civil disturbance which shuts down oil production. Perhaps that is why the US armed forces have formed an "African Command" and the European countries were so quick to engage with the Arab Spring. At least, increasingly unstable Egypt is no longer a worry; it has become a net oil importer. Syria is not far behind, with its oil exports declining well before the current civil war started. [1]

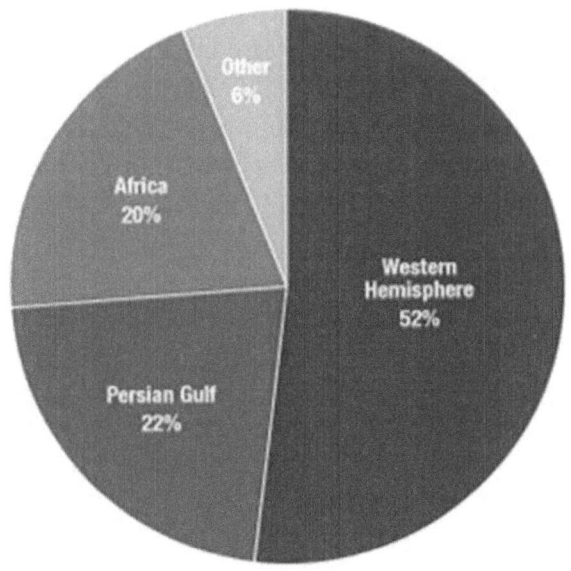

Global oil production. [1]

2.1. Global crude oil production

Global crude oil production from 1989 to the end of 2014 is shown in the Fig. World oil output reached about 89 million barrels per day (b/d) in 2014, an increase of 2.1 million b/d compared to 2013, all of which was in non-

---

([1])Roger Boyd: Energy and the Financial System Springer Cham Heidelberg New York Dordrecht London 2013. P 32

([1])Iakovos Alhadeff: USA Russia & China in the Middle East. Free ebook.net 2014. P 6

OPEC countries. US output grew by 1.6 million b/d, its largest increase on record. This is due to supplies of shale oil and will continue to increase over the next decade. Nonetheless, as depicted in the Fig, 60% of total global oil was produced by NOCs in 2015.

The Figure presents the worldwide oil consumption trend for the period 1989–2014. In 2014, global consumption was around 92 million b/d, an increase of 840,000 b/d compared to 2013, with the emerging economies accounting for all of the net increase. [1]

---

[1]Michael Ala: The Imperial College Lectures in PETROLEUM ENGINEERING. World Scientific Publishing Europe Ltd. 2017. P 221

Economics of oil and gas production

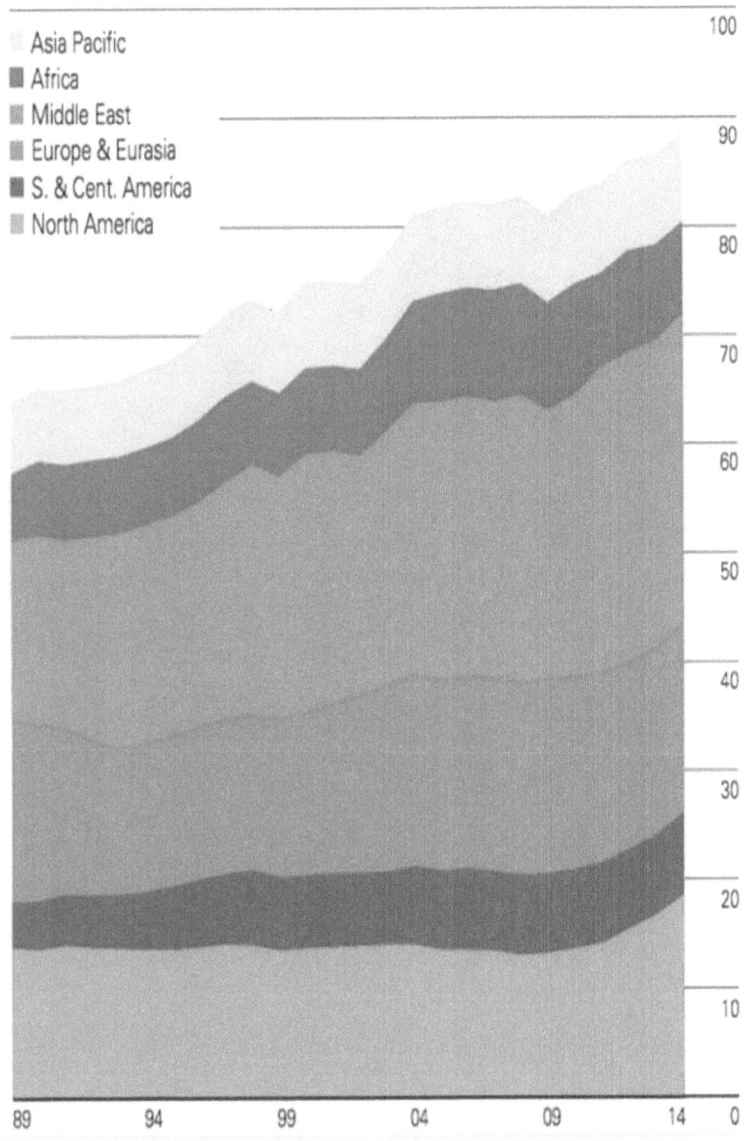

2000	2015
World: 75,166 thousand barrels/day	**World: 91,863** thousand barrels/day

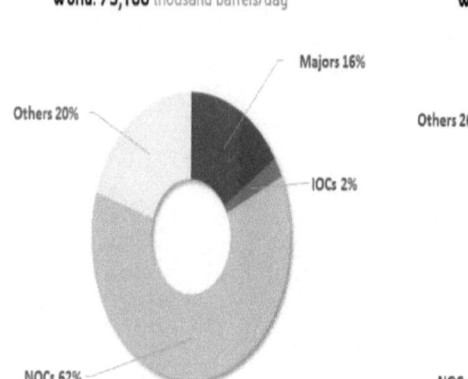
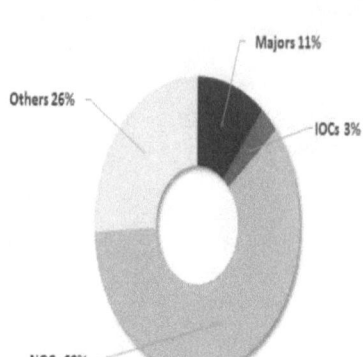

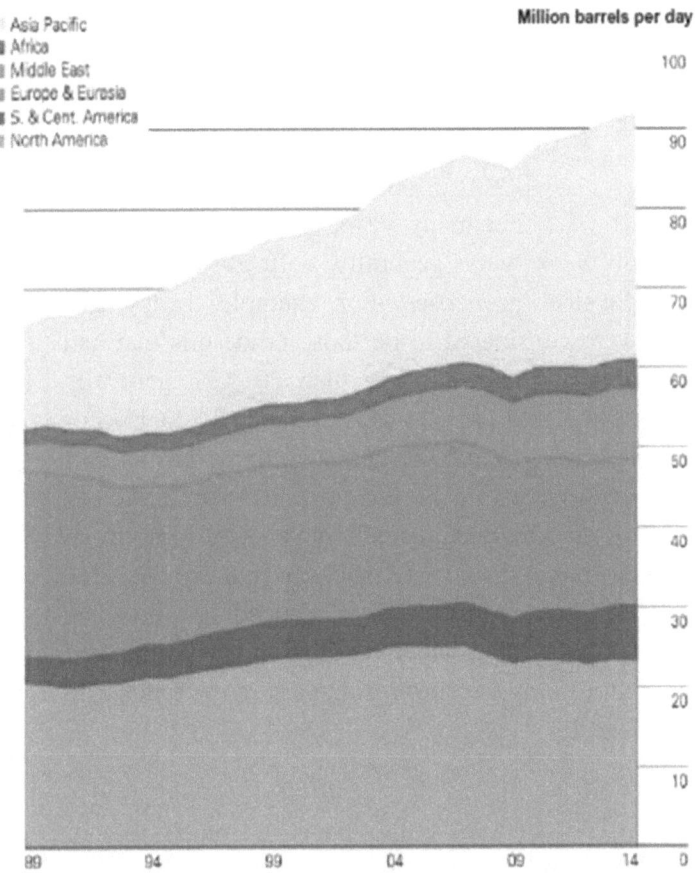

2.2. Biological Upgrading of Heavy Crudes

Heavy oils are more difficult to recover from the subsurface reservoir than light oils. The definition of heavy oils is usually based on the API gravity or viscosity, and the definition is quite arbitrary although there have been attempts to rationalize the definition based on viscosity, API gravity, and density.

For many years, petroleum and heavy oil were very generally defined in terms of physical properties. For example, heavy oils were considered to be those crude oils that had gravity somewhat less than 20 API, generally falling into the API gravity range 10 to 15. For example, Cold Lake heavy crude oil has an API gravity equal to 12 and extra heavy oils, such as tar sand bitumen, usually have an API gravity in the range 5 to 10 (Athabasca bitumen=8 API). Residua would vary depending on the temperature at which distillation was terminated but usually vacuum residua are in the range 2 to 8 API.

Heavy oils have a much higher viscosity (and lower API gravity) than conventional petroleum, and primary recovery of these petroleum types usually requires thermal stimulation of the reservoir. The generic term heavy oil is often applied to a crude oil that has less than 20 API and usually, but not always, a sulfur content higher than 2% by weight. Further, in contrast to conventional crude oils, heavy oils are darker in color and may even be black.

The term heavy oil has also been arbitrarily used to describe both the heavy oils that require thermal stimulation of recovery from the reservoir and the bitumen in bituminous sand formations from which the heavy bituminous material is recovered by mining operation.

Extra heavy oils are materials that occur in the solid or near-solid state and are generally incapable of free flow under reservoir conditions. [1]

The expected increase in the production of heavy and extra-heavy crude oils has led oil companies to develop new technologies in order to improve their properties, as well as to facilitate their recovery and transportation. Chemical and thermal methods commonly used are expensive and troublesome, which together with the increasing environmental restrictions resulted in an increased interest in the application of biological treatments to reduce the viscosity and density of unconventional crude oils, as a cheaper and environmentally friendly alternative or as a complementary technology. [2]

---

[1] James G. Speight: The Chemistry and Technology of Petroleum. FOURTH EDITION. Taylor & Francis Group, LLC. 2007. P 50

[2] Kirsten Heimann • Obulisamy Parthiba Karthikeyan

For instance, solvents are usually employed to reduce the viscosity of heavy crude oils and help in their recovery and transportation. These chemical compounds could be replaced by biosurfactants, surface-active compounds synthesized by microorganisms, which can perform the same function and, due to their biological origin, are less toxic and more easily biodegradable, thus implying a greater environmental compatibility.

Special attention has been paid to the biological upgrading of heavy and extra-heavy crude oils, the goal of which is to improve their value and make them easier to produce, transport and process. The reactions that could improve the properties of heavy crude oils include cleavage of large aliphatic chains, aromatic rings, heterocycles, resins and asphaltene molecules into smaller compounds to reduce the average molecular weight of crude oil and, at the same time, modify their interactions with other molecules, resulting in the rearrangement of aggregates to liberate the smaller trapped molecules. As a result, the viscosity of the oil is reduced and its flow properties are improved, which enhances the mobility of crude oil through the reservoirs and the pipelines. [1]

Subramanian Senthilkannan Muthu: Biodegradation and Bioconversion of Hydrocarbons. Springer Science+Business Media Singapore 2017. P 342: 343
[1]Kirsten Heimann • Obulisamy Parthiba Karthikeyan

Despite some promising results achieved in bioconversion of heavy oil fractions using different microorganisms, a limiting factor is that long incubation times are required, in most cases about 15–60 days or more. The bioconversion of crude oil's heaviest components (such as asphaltenes) using whole cells is difficult, due to their low solubility and low mass transfer rates in aqueous systems (where the microbial activity usually takes place), and the difficulty of their transportation across the cell membrane, which results in low transformation rates. Therefore, it is desirable the development of biotechnological processes that can upgrade heavy and extra-heavy oils in a one phase, non-aqueous system. Enzymes require less water than microorganisms to perform their catalytic activity. In this case, crude oil itself can act as a reaction matrix, thus avoiding or minimizing the addition of water, and consequently increasing the solubility and the bioavailability of hydrophobic substrates. The ability of enzymes of working in the absence of water or with very low amounts of water represents an advantage when compared with the use of microorganisms for crude oil upgrading. [1]

Subramanian Senthilkannan Muthu: Biodegradation and Bioconversion of Hydrocarbons. Springer Science+Business Media Singapore 2017. P 343

[1] Kirsten Heimann • Obulisamy Parthiba Karthikeyan Subramanian Senthilkannan Muthu: Biodegradation and Bioconversion of Hydrocarbons. Springer

2.3. Offshore oil production

Offshore oil industry discharges consist of three separate sources: oil spills, discharges of oil from drill muds and cuttings, and discharges in association with PW. Unlike accidental oil spillage, oil in PW is permitted subject to regulatory control at national and European levels. It should be noted that discharge of OBM practically ceased from 1st January 1997 when legislative levels of oil at 10 g/kg were technically not achievable. Discharges from offshore O&G activity rose steeply in the 1980–1986 period, and then stabilized and declined, in spite of increasing production, mainly as a result of voluntary and legislative action to reduce and ban usage of OBM. The types of mineral oil lost from offshore operations are dominated by crude oil (43 % of volume and 54 % of incidents), diesel/fuel oils (34 % volume and 20 % incidents), and base oil (17 % volume and 1.3 % incidents). The remainder include hydraulic oil (1.8 % volume), graphite grease (1 % volume), condensate (0.7 % volume), and lube oil (0.25 % volume). Almost 7 % of incidents involved unknown material (2.7 % volume). OBM dominated the *28,000 t/year inputs of oil from the North Sea offshore industry from 1984 until 1988. Releases from spills and flaring were also significant in

1986 and 1988. Between 1989 and 1991, oil inputs were lower (from 17,000 to 21,000 t/year) and consisted of OBM and PW in combination. Between 1992 and 1996 oil in PW became dominant with inputs ranging from 10,000 to 14,000 t/year. In 1997, oil inputs were still 17,000 t due to increasing PW volumes as fields aged, and also due to use of synthetic drilling muds. [1]

2.4. Shale Oil

Oil shale is an organic-rich fine-grained sedimentary rock containing significant amounts of kerogen (a solid mixture of organic chemical compounds) from which technology can extract liquid hydrocarbons (shale oil) and combustible oil shale gas. [2]

Oil shale deposits are found in all world oil provinces, although most of them are too deep to be exploited economically. The kerogen in oil shale can be converted to shale oil through the chemical processes of pyrolysis

[1] Kirsten Heimann • Obulisamy Parthiba Karthikeyan Subramanian Senthilkannan Muthu: Biodegradation and Bioconversion of Hydrocarbons. Springer Science+Business Media Singapore 2017. P 16: 17

[2] Patrick A. Narbel · Jan Petter Hansen Jan R. Lien: Energy Technologies and Economics. Springer International Publishing Switzerland 2014. P 113

(decomposition by heating), hydrogenation, or thermal dissolution. The temperature when perceptible decomposition of oil shale occurs depends on the time-scale of the pyrolysis; in the above ground retorting process the perceptible decomposition occurs at 300° C but proceeds more rapidly and completely at higher temperatures. The ratio of shale gas to shale oil depends on the retorting temperature and as a rule increases with the rise in temperature.

Modern in-situ process, which involves heating the oil shale underground, may take several months of heating, decomposition may be conducted as low as 250 °C. Such technologies can potentially extract more oil from a given area of land than ex-situ processes, since they can access the material at greater depths than surface mines can. Oil shale has also been burnt directly as a low-grade fuel.

Depending on the exact properties of oil shale and the exact processing technology, the retorting process may be water and energy extensive. A critical measure of the viability of extraction of shale oil lies in the ratio of the energy produced by the oil shale to the energy used in its mining and processing, a ratio known as "Energy Returned on Energy Invested" (EROEI). A 1984 study estimated the EROEI of the various known oil-shale deposits as varying between 0.7–13.3. Global technically recoverable oil shale reserves are substantial with the largest reserves in the United States, Russia and Brazil. However, the production of shale oil is very limited compared to conventional oil production from sandstone and chalk reservoirs. The most important producers are Estonia, Brazil, China, and to some extent Germany and Russia. Oil shale gains attention as a potential abundant source of oil whenever the price of crude oil rises. At the same time, oil-shale mining and processing raise a number of environmental concerns, such as land use, waste disposal, water use, waste-water management, greenhouse-gas emissions and air pollution. The reserves of oil shale are large, estimated to about 4.8 trillion barrels. The economics of extracting this resource strongly limit its attractiveness for the time being. [1]

Extraction of oil and gas from shale formations has become a technically and economically viable complement to conventional oil production only within a decade. The great increase in shale oil production observed over the past couple of years, driven by high oil prices and new technology, was unforeseen by most analysts,

---

[1]Patrick A. Narbel ·Jan Petter Hansen Jan R. Lien: Energy Technologies and Economics. Springer International Publishing Switzerland 2014. P 114

and the initial estimates of potential production rates have already been surpassed in the USA (EIA2008; IEA2010). The development of horizontal drilling and advanced hydraulic fracturing (fracking) of shale formations has led to what has been described as a revolution in energy production in North America.

Total US oil production has increased significantly (EIA2014a), and shale oil now makes up almost half of total US oil production (EIA 2014b). The shale revolution in North America has been an eye-opener for the rest of the world regarding the possibilities for development of shale oil production. Analysts are now attempting to generate resource estimates for shale regions around the world and to project potential future production from these places, in the hope that the American shale revolution can be repeated elsewhere.

So far, the most promising regions of technically recoverable resources outside of North America have been identified in Russia, China, Argentina and Libya (EIA2013). However, some researchers also warn that recent estimates of contingent resources of shale oil and gas are too high. [1]

---

[1] Henrik Wachtmeister, Linnea Lund, Kjell Aleklett, and Mikael Hook. Production Decline Curves of Tight Oil Wells in Eagle Ford Shale. Natural Resources Research.

Production of tight oil wells declines fast, on average 74, 47 and 19% annually for the first, second and third year of production, respectively, based on investigated data from the Eagle Ford formation.

These numbers broadly agree with Hughes (2014), study on Eagle Ford and Bakken. Hyperbolic and stretched exponential curve fit models can be used to model this production behavior. [1]

The USA possesses nearly 62 % of the potentially recoverable world oil shale resources. US oil shale presents enormous potential for domestic energy production. Whereas total oil resources in the contiguous USA are estimated at 47.5 billion barrels and undiscovered and technically recoverable oil resources are estimated at 6.2 billion barrels at ten sites in western states, the US Geological Survey (USGS) estimates total US oil shale resources at 2.1 trillion barrels. Testimony made before the Senate Oil Shale Energy and Natural Resources Committee termed US oil shale potential as "staggering". An estimated 750 billion barrels of

---

2017. P 1
([1])Henrik Wachtmeister, Linnea Lund, Kjell Aleklett, and Mikael Hook. Production Decline Curves of Tight Oil Wells in Eagle Ford Shale. Natural Resources Research. 2017. P 12

shale oil could be recovered from North America's oil shale resource base with currently available technology and, ultimately, more than one trillion barrels may be recovered.

From the perspective of near-term energy independence, however, oil shale will offset a relatively small proportion of US demand for oil. In 2002, the USA consumed 10.5 million barrels per day (mmbd) of imported oil. Consumption is projected to reach 29.2 mmbd by 2023, at which time US oil shale production rates of 2 mmbd might be achieved. Ultimate capacity, however, could reach 10 mmbd.

Future commercial oil shale production relies on industry investments, which are by no means assured. Thus, in the near term, oil shale will make only modest contributions to US energy independence. [1]

([1])J. Edward Gates • David L. Trauger • Brian Czech: Peak Oil, Economic Growth, and Wildlife Conservation. Springer Science+Business Media New York 2014. P 246: 247

Economics of oil and gas production

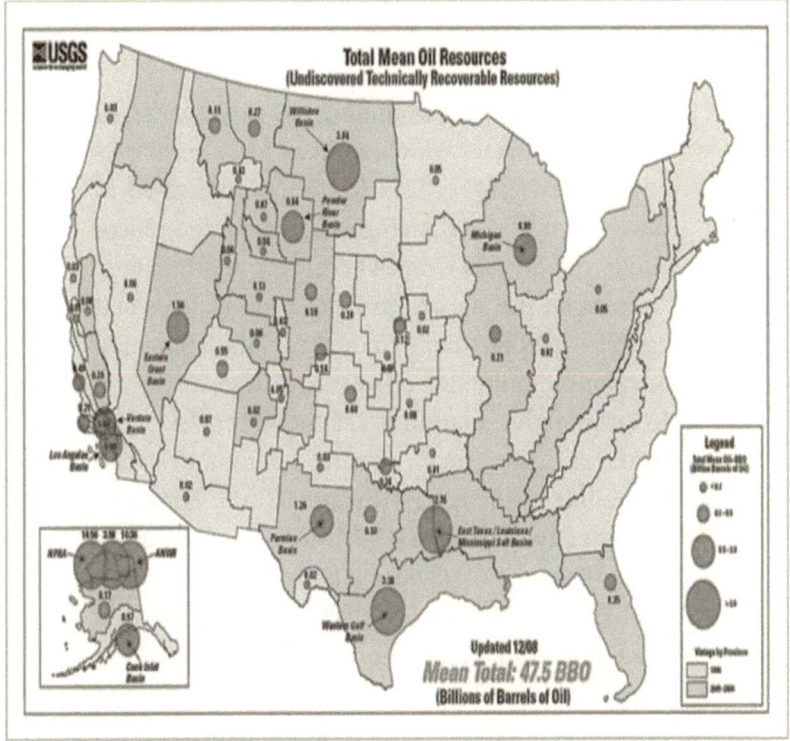

3. Gas production

The most common gas component of NGH is methane, which appears to be primarily of biogenic origin. This has been confirmed in passive continental margins such as the Blake Ridge off the SE U.S., where deep thermogenic sources do not appear to have been tapped, and carbon isotope data indicates that biogenic methane dominates (Paull and Ussler 2001). Even in active margin areas, however, biogenic methane is much more common than thermogenic methane (Kastner 2001). Biogenic gas directly feeding GHSZ has been observed in drill holes (Wellsbury and Parkes 2003; Wellsbury et al. 2001; Wellsbury et al. 2000). Of the many drill holes into oceanic NGH, only a few have more than a few percent of thermogenic gas or traces of liquid hydrocarbons (Kvenvolden 1988). Where deeper hydrocarbon sources are tapped by deep faults, thermogenic gas may be a locally prominent component of the gas mixture along with traces of liquid petroleum.

Such deep faulting is common in accretionary margins such as Cascadia (Trehu et al. 2004). Natural gas liquids (NGL) of higher carbon number gases such as ethane, propane, and butane that might be expected to form under GHSZ pressure and temperature conditions have not been observed in association with petroleumrelated thermogenic NGH. The NGL will not be present so long as there is water for them to react with. These gases have a stronger preference for forming NGH than methane, and complete sequestration of them in compound NGH in the presence of water is the rule. NGH is rarely associated with liquid hydrocarbons, even when the gas has a thermogenic source, although in some rare cases, where a very active conventional petroleum system leaks to the seabed, NGH and liquid petroleum may occur together, as has been observed locally in the Gulf of Mexico.

Passive margins without deep faulting that could tap a thermogenic deep petroleum system, such as exist on the basin/continental margins of both the Amerasia and Eurasia Basins in the High Arctic, appear to be overwhelmingly sourced by biogenic methane. The NGH concentrations can be expected to be of high purity.

This could be important to opening NGH exploration and production in the Arctic Ocean because the risk of pollution in the event of an accident that might release some gas is extremely low.

Apart from gas that can be observed naturally venting from the seafloor, the presence of bottom-simulating reflectors (BSRs) on seismic sections is a first order evidence for natural gas production and retention, but BSRs give little direct evidence about the potential for NGH concentrations. A BSR is useful only in the very early stages of exploration. The BSR is a reflection at a negative acoustic impedance contrast caused by free gas in the sediment below NGH in the GHSZ.

Acoustic impedance is calculated as the product of compressional wave velocity times density; an acoustic reflection is produced at any interface where a contrast in acoustic impedance exists.

The presence of gas below the BSR markedly lowers the velocity and the gas NGH above increases the velocity somewhat compared to water-saturated sediments.

A BSR does not mean that a gas column above water is present, especially in muddy sediments with low permeability where diffusion may be the primary mechanism of gas migration. Where an inclined permeable horizon crosses into a GHSZ, however, it is common to find gas pooled below NGH in pore space.

Depending on the thickness of the permeable horizons, velocity analysis can be used to estimate both the NGH saturation and gas-water relationship. Estimates of leakage at the seafloor combined with gas and NGH in-place will allow estimates of gas flux to be made. A first order of approximation for adequate gas flux, however, will be provided by the existence of the NGH itself. If gas flux were not high enough, no NGH would form.

Even in the lower portion of the GHSZ, however, NGH concentrations with no BSR have been observed. This appears to have occurred when pore water solutions in the sediments immediately below NGH-enriched strata have been undersaturated with respect to gas generation so that no free gas is present.

However, in the observed case, the saturation was apparently high enough to provide a driving force for NGH crystallization once the solutions reached the GHSZ. NGH concentrations can also form well above the base of the GHSZ from solutions that were relatively undersaturated and in which the driving force for NGH crystallization was too low until they have migrated to shallower depths where saturation increases as a function of lower pressure and where temperature is colder. These higher-level NGH concentrations will be indistinguishable from deposits formed from solutions formed lower in the GHSZ because the conditions governing crystallization will be the same.

In lower-grade deposits that tend to be finer grained (muddier) and less well bed-differentiated, continuous BSRs often occur at approximately the location of the base of the GHSZ and may extend over large areas. BSRs, whose importance has been overemphasized in the past, often constitute first order features on seismic sections. These well-defined BSRs, such as are seen in the Blake Ridge area of the U.S. East Coast continental margin, are dramatic seismic features but are of limited exploration and economic value beyond identifying the region as a gas province. The NGH associated with these features often forms extremely large, low-grade deposits (Max et al. 2006) that have relatively small percentages of between 3 % and 8 % NGH in diffusely defined horizons throughout huge volumes of fairly uniform muddy sediments. These do not constitute primary exploration targets.

The total amount of biogenic gas at a typical sedimentary site results from a cumulative process that potentially may have gone on over a long period of time.

Methane is created by bacteria in sediments within and below the GHSZ, but at temperatures lower than the 'oil window'. Where gas is formed below the GHSZ, it will tend to rise as bubbles and by diffusion. When it enters the GHSZ it can react with water to form NGH. As sedimentation goes on, new sediment will bury older strata. Heat flow will tend to remain the same, so the thermal gradient beneath the sea floor will remain constant, as the GHSZ will maintain a nearly constant thickness during sedimentation. The result is that isotherms will rise to accommodate the accumulating strata because any given isotherm will maintain a constant sub-bottom depth below the surface. Pressure, which is dependent on water depth, will not change much, so the warming of deeper strata as isotherms rise to maintain the thermal structure of the GHSZ causes an upward migration of the base of the GHSZ. The upward migration of the base of the GHSZ through the sediments will result in dissociation of previously formed NGH that had been at the base of the GHSZ. The released gas will migrate upward, nourishing formation of new NGH in the superjacent GHSZ. This combined process of formation of new biogenic gas and recycling of basal GHSZ NGH will have the effect of increasing the amount of NGH in deposits and can go on as long as sedimentary accretion (including organic carbon) continues. Deep gas does not need to be sourced so long as the sediment/NGH accumulation system at depths less than the depth of the oil window functions appropriately. [1]

Methane occurs naturally due to the biological decomposition of organic matter available on the earth's surface and is frequently manifested as marsh gas from wastelands, ponds, etc. Large gas reserves under the earth have been detected where methane exists as crystals (gas hydrates) formed due to the interaction with water and methane molecules as a clathrate compound at high pressure and low temperature, usually below 20°C. Because of the abundance of methane gas formed in the geological period under the earth's surface, usually in the Arctic region below the sea bed which is enough to saturate water at a very low temperature, methane hydrates are formed. Gas hydrates have been found at depths of 200 m to 1,000 m in the sea. Below this depth, ice layers, permafrost (permanent frost), of water is prevalent. The temperature of sea water decreases as depth increases and the rate of decreases in temperature with respect to the depth is known as hydrothermal gradient. While the geothermal temperature below the sea bed increases at a rate of 34°C per km. Thus, gas hydrates exist only a few hundred meters below

---

[1] Michael D. Max · Arthur H. Johnson William P. Dillon: Natural Gas Hydrate – Arctic Ocean Deepwater Resource Potential. 2013. P 35: 38

the sea bed where the temperature is below 20°C and after this depth it cannot exist because of higher temperature due to geothermal conditions. Gas hydrates are lighter than water once dislodged from the bulk it floats on the sea water and gradually releases methane from the sea surface. Hydrates are stable up to a maximum temperature of 15°C. Hence, if the temperature increases above 15°C, gas will be released from the hydrate. In fact, other hydrocarbon gases, such as ethane, propane, butane, carbon dioxide, and helium, may also be present in the hydrates along with methane. The presence of these gases also contributes to the stability of gas hydrates in a range of temperatures. Hydrate reserves are identified by the seismic exploration method.

Approximately, 164 Nm^3 of methane is available from 1 m^3 of gas hydrate containing 0.2 m^3 of gas and 0.8 m^3 of water. Exploration is carried out during winter while the sub-sea level is favorable for stable gas hydrates in the reserve. [1]

---

[1] Uttam Ray Chaudhuri: Fundamentals of Petroleum and Petrochemical Engineering. Taylor and Francis Group. 2011. P 20: 21

3.1. Gas production method

A well is drilled and hot water is introduced to release the gas. But propagation of heat through the well to the reserve will cause the release of gases from the surroundings of the well, as a result a special type of dome-shaped collecting device is used. Methane is traced by infrared (IR) sensor. A schematic production method is presented in Figure. The economics of the production is dependent on the cost of energy supply for generating hot water by burning a part of the recovered gas and cost of collection. The ratio of heating value of methane to the heat required to release methane per cubic meter of hydrate is a good indication of the economic viability of such a production method. Compressed carbon dioxide as the product of combustion in this process is injected back into the reserve to replenish the gas collected. Since gas hydrates are available in the deep-sea area, exploration and production require huge investments and operating expenses. Storage of methane and its transportation are also troublesome due to gas hydrate formation. In a pipe transfer under the sea or low temperature area, methanol is injected to avoid hydrate formation at the prevailing temperature. Though large amounts of gas hydrate reserve are available in the permafrost zone, it is difficult to produce with the existing technology. [1]

3.2. Global natural gas production

As a clean and low-carbon energy resource, natural gas is considered to be relatively superior and has drawn increasing attention in recent years. China, India, Brazil, and other gas-poor developing countries have been inclined to increasingly use it as an end-use energy resource. However, even though natural gas in the developed countries is a widely used heating fuel and its share in terms of energy end use is high, its share has shown little growth in the past 40 years. This is because natural gas in these countries is mainly used for electricity generation. [1]

The measurement of gas production is even more confused by the varying treatment of the non-combustible components, such as carbon dioxide or nitrogen which are present in some fields. The amounts flared, re-injected into the reservoir and used to fuel the facilities are also not consistently reported. A liquid, known as *condensate*, condenses naturally from gas at surface conditions of temperature and pressure,

---

[1]Uttam Ray Chaudhuri: Fundamentals of Petroleum and Petrochemical Engineering. Taylor and Francis Group. 2011. P 22
[1]Yi-Ming Wei • Hua Liao: Energy Economics: Energy Efficiency in China. Springer International Publishing Switzerland 2016. P 24

and may be treated as ordinary oil for most purposes. In addition, *natural gas liquids* (NGL), mainly pentane and butane, are produced at dedicated plants which may draw their supplies from a number of different fields, making it difficult to attribute the production to the fields concerned. Gas itself may be liquefied at very low temperature for transport from remote locations, being known as *liquefied natural gas*, with the easily confused acronym of *LNG*. [1]

Gas is an essential component of the EU energy mix, constituting one quarter of primary energy supply and contributing mainly to electricity generation, heating, feedstock for industry and fuel for transportation. Since the dawn of the European gas industry in 1959, EU domestic gas production has progressively grown over time. Th is growth was mainly due to the North Sea, a fact that explains the high domestic production of the Netherlands and the UK.

In particular, EU domestic gas production has largely benefited, from the mid-1990s to the mid-2000s, from the high level of gas production in the UK. However, the UK gas

---

[1] C.J. Campbell: Campbell's Atlas of Oil and Gas Depletion. Colin J. Campbell and Alexander Wöstmann 2013. P 12

production fell very dramatically over the last decade, from 108 billion cubic meters (Bcm) in 2000 to 37 Bcm in 2014. This declining trend is set to continue into the future. Government's scenarios illustrate that production will decline further in the 2020s, to reach about 20 Bcm in 2030. It should be noted that a significant share of future gas production is expected to come from new fields. Considering the current low oil and gas prices environment, investing in the development of these new fields might well turn out to be challenging for oil and gas companies. Th is might add further uncertainty to the future outlook of gas production in the UK.

In the Netherlands, gas production dropped from 70 Bcm in 2010 to 56 Bcm in 2014. Th e country's government decided, in early 2014, to cap the production at the large Groningen gas field following earthquakes in the production region. Limits on Groningen production were initially set at 42.5 Bcm for 2015 and 2016 and at 40 Bcm for 2016. However, in December 2015, the government ultimately decided to further limit the extraction at Groningen, to a level of 27 Bcm for the 2015/2016 gas year. While taking this decision, the government also outlined its intention to further reduce long-term production levels at the gas field, possibly to a level between 18 and 24 Bcm in 2020. In this framework, a further gas production decline in the Netherlands will be unavoidable in coming years. Furthermore, it should be outlined that Groningen has always played a very important role of swing producer in continental North-western Europe. Th e reduced future output of the field could thus put into question this role, therefore reducing the overall flexibility of European gas markets. [1]

In sum, over the next decades, EU domestic gas production will continue its downward trajectory. However, there is a great uncertainty about the steepness of this decline, as this will also depend on the potential production of shale gas in the EU, and most notably in the UK and Poland. Over the last few years, expectations have indeed emerged in the EU about the opportunity of rebalancing the declining conventional gas production story with a new, potential, unconventional gas production narrative. However, these expectations have soon proved to be illusory, due to disappointing test wells, regulatory constraints, and continued public hostility. Moratoria forbidding unconventional gas extraction was adopted in different countries both *de jure* (e.g. France, Bulgaria, the Netherlands) and *de facto* (e.g. Germany). Th ese constrains have added to deteriorating economics as a result of lower oil

---

[1]Simone Tagliapietra: Energy Relations in the Euro-Mediterranean. 2017. P 43: 45

and gas prices that have all contributed to dimming the outlook for unconventional gas in the EU, even in the case of the one regarded as the most promising unconventional gas hotspot in the EU: Poland. In this country, eight of the 11 international oil and gas companies, which had invested in the sector, indeed, halted their exploration activities by end-2015.

As far as the EU gas demand is concerned, the trend has generally been on the rise over the last few decades. In fact, the EU gas demand grew on average by 4.2 percent during the 1990s, and by 2 percent from 2000 to 2008. EU gas demand strongly decreased in 2009 for the first time, primarily because of global financial turmoil; in 2010, it bounced back, reaching a new all-time high of 502 Bcm, mainly because of a slight economic recovery and a cold winter. However, in 2011, the EU gas demand experienced a new decrease (453 Bcm), due to the worsening of the economic crisis and a mild winter. Th is trend has further worsened in 2014, as the EU gas demand reached a level of 387 Bcm: the lowest since 1995. Th e economic crisis, subdued demand for electricity and changes in the electricity production sector, with the growing role of solid fuels (mainly coal) and renewables, are all factors behind this drop. [1]

---

[1]Simone Tagliapietra: Energy Relations in the Euro-

Norway has always been a reliable gas supplier to the EU, but some concerns are emerging about its capability to deliver its gas supply in the long-term. Th e oil output of Norway peaked in 2000. As tax revenues from hydrocarbon extraction represent an important share of Norway's state budget, the declining oil output over the last decade was one of the driving forces behind Norway's impressive gas development. Norway exported, in 2014, about 100 Bcm of gas, almost twice the amount of a decade ago. However, it is a matter of fact that Norway has not made a significant gas discovery since the discovery of the Ormen Langen field in 1997. Th is field, originally assessed at 400 Bcm, has also been successively downgraded to 220 Bcm. [1]

Although natural gas had been used for many centuries, interest in it as an energy source began only at the beginning of the 20th century. An important energy source requires a distribution system which was lacking for natural gas until the 1940s. Pipeline construction began in the United States then and continued into the 1960s. As a result, gas could be easily and cheaply delivered to many remote parts of the country. A similar phenomenon took place in Europe.

Mediterranean. 2017. P 45: 46
[1]Simone Tagliapietra: Energy Relations in the Euro-Mediterranean. 2017. P 54

Some countries, such as Japan, had not yet developed any indigenous sources and found it too expensive to build pipelines. They developed a trade with Indonesia in liquid natural gas. By the 1970s, natural gas was a major energy fuel. It became so popular that shortages appeared in the market and its price rose. In the late 1970s and into the 1980s the production of oil in the United States stabilized. This was an important cause of the shortages because oil production had been its most important source. [1]

Worldwide natural gas production during the period 1989–2014 is shown in the Fig. Global natural gas output reached 3,461 billion cubic meters (BCM) in 2014, an increase of 1.6% compared to 2013.

With an increase of 6.1%, the US remained the world's leading producer. In the case of gas, the global production shares of the NOCs and non-state sector each amounted to 49% in 2015.

The global natural gas consumption trend for the period 1989– 2014 is shown in the

---

[1] Sidney Borowitz: FAREWELL FOSSIL FUELS Reviewing America' s. Energy Policy. Plenum Press, New York in 1999. P 73: 74

Fig. In 2014, global gas consumption amounted to 3,393.0 BCM, an increase of 0.4% over 2013, with the US and China recording the largest growth. [1]

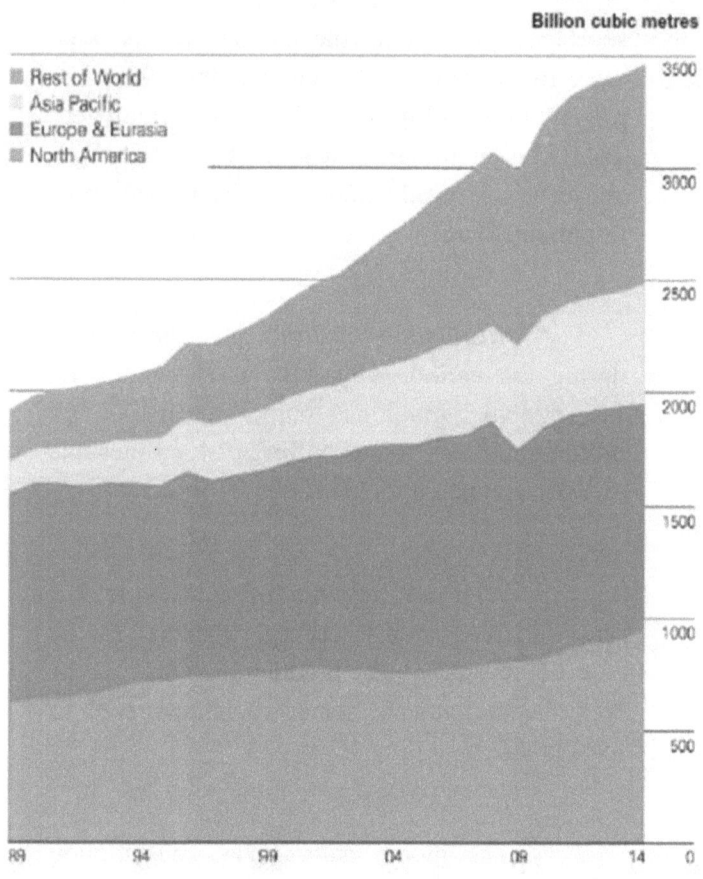

([1])Michael Ala: The Imperial College Lectures in PETROLEUM ENGINEERING. World Scientific Publishing Europe Ltd. 2017. P 221:224

Economics of oil and gas production

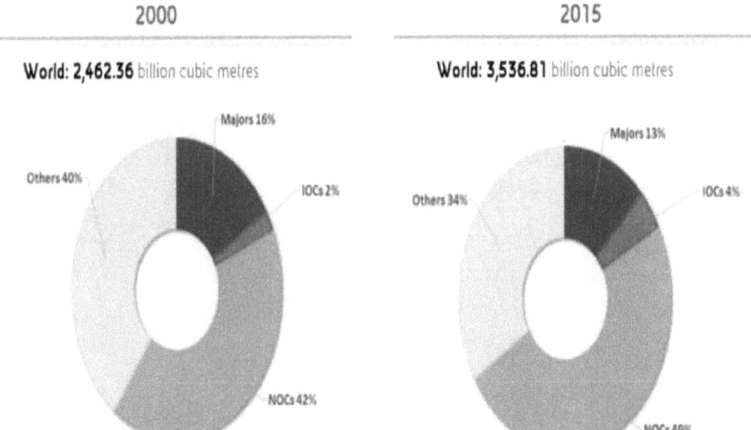

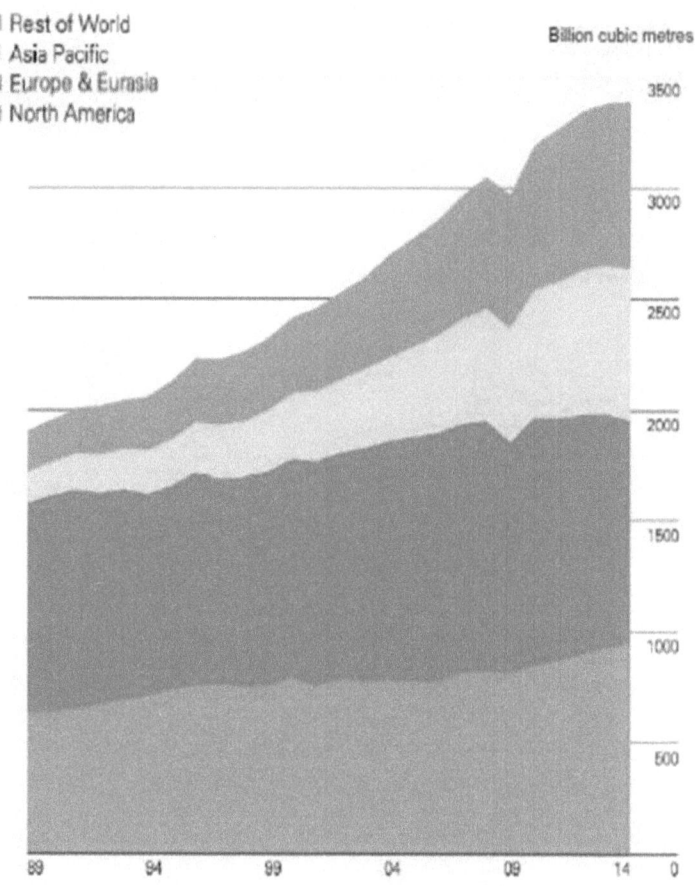

3.3. Natural Gas: EROI 10:1 and Declining; 23.7 % of Energy Usage

Natural Gas supplies 23.7 % of global energy usage and has a current global EROI of about 10:1 for conventional gas fields. It was first treated as a useless by-product of oil extraction, being "flared off" at the well site. No one has documented how much natural gas was wasted in this way, but the amounts must have been huge. The use of natural gas has grown rapidly over the past few decades. It is increasingly being used for space heating, cooking, generating electricity, and in the production of synthetic fertilizers. The latter use played a large part in the postwar "Green Revolution" which facilitated the rapid growth of populations in many countries. Being a gas at room temperature NG is primarily moved overland via pipelines. To transport NG by sea it has to be cooled to −162° C at which point it becomes a liquid that can be carried in specially engineered liquid natural gas (LNG) ships. This is an expensive process which offsets some of the energy provided by the natural gas thus transported. These comparative factors support the construction of pipelines over many thousands of miles between Russian production fields and Europe via the Ukraine and Poland. Despite these limitations, LNG has grown rapidly to become a quarter of the global natural gas export market.

Presently many countries with large NG supplies cannot utilize it all, a number of richer countries have heavily depleted their fields, and there are large pricing discrepancies between regional markets separated by water. It is currently two to three times as expensive to buy natural gas in Europe as it is in North America while prices in the Far East are even higher. One possibility in "gas rich" countries is to use LNG as a transport fuel to replace oil, a strategy which has been successfully used in buses, trucks, and ships. This could definitely be an option to reduce the impact of declining cheap oil reserves, providing some more time for society to find alternative fuels and living arrangements. On the other hand, if such substitution was applied extensively it would significantly increase the demand for natural gas and thus speed up depletion of positive net energy reserves. [1]

In the next 10–15 years, significant increases in global natural gas production are possible. However, the net energy of many of the newer supplies is significantly less than the

[1] Roger Boyd: Energy and the Financial System Springer Cham Heidelberg New York Dordrecht London 2013. P 17: 18

older fields so increases in net energy will lag increases in gross production volumes. LNG can also be used as a substitute for oil as a transport fuel, especially for buses, trucks, and ships. Royal Dutch Shell is chartering two river barges which are designed to run on LNG and is also planning to provide LNG fuel stops along a truck route in Alberta, Canada. If such uses become widespread, they may soften the blow of falling oil production, but greater gas usage will certainly speed up the depletion of natural gas reserves. With the increasing impacts of climate change any increases in production may also be limited by external constraints put in place to limit the amount of heat-trapping gases emitted into the atmosphere. The very high short-term climate impact of methane, together with environmental issues affecting shale gas production, may mean that natural gas production comes under the same level of citizen resistance currently impacting coal production. [1]

Natural gas production provides about 24 % of global energy usage. The outlook is for at least another decade of increasing natural gas production, but with probable reductions in EROI as more remote and difficult-to-produce deposits are utilized. The increasing

---

[1] Roger Boyd: Energy and the Financial System Springer Cham Heidelberg New York Dordrecht London 2013. P 35

transportation of liquefied natural gas (LNG) by ship also results in a reduction of the net energy available as it consumes more than 10 % of the energy embodied in the gas being transported. Coal production, which provides the balance of the fossil fuel supply, has increased rapidly in the past decade. The outlook is for continuing increases in coal production, but a likely reduction of net energy as lesser grades, and deeper deposits of coal, are used. As touched on above, the peak production of coal and gas may arrive sooner as oil supplies dwindle and all stages of exploration, extraction and transportation become more and more expensive. [1]

3.4. Gas sales profiles; influence of contracts

If the gas purchaser is a company which distributes gas to domestic and industrial end users, he typically wants the producer to provide:

_ a guaranteed minimum quantity of gas for as long duration as possible (for ease of planning and the comfort of being able to guarantee supply to the end user) and

[1] Roger Boyd: Energy and the Financial System Springer Cham Heidelberg New York Dordrecht London 2013. P 52

_ peaks in production when required (e.g. when the weather unexpectedly turns cold).

The better the producer can meet these two requirements, the higher the price paid by the purchaser is likely to be.

In contrast to an oil production profile, which typically has a plateau period of 2–5 years, a gas field production profile will typically have a much longer plateau period, producing around 2/3 of the reserves on plateau production in order to satisfy the needs of the distribution company to forecast their supplies. The Figure compares typical oil and gas field production profiles.

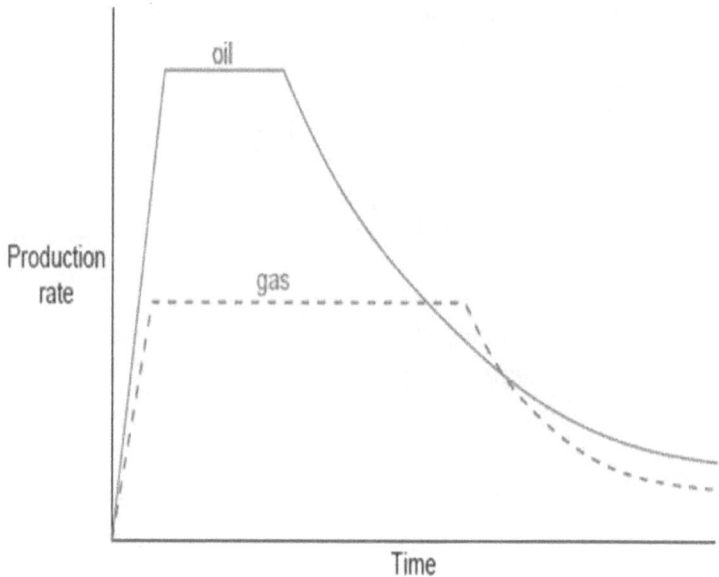

If the distribution of gas in a country is run by a nationalized or state-owned company, there is effectively a monopoly on this service, and prices for gas distributed through a grid system will have to be negotiated with the distribution company. If the market for distribution is not regulated then opportunities arise to sell gas to other customers and directly to consumers, perhaps including a tariff payment for transport through a national grid.

This situation has arisen in the UK where competition for gas sales has been encouraged. Gas producers can enter into direct agreements with consumers (ranging from power stations to domestic users), using the national distribution grid if necessary. Such a deregulated market increases competition between the distribution companies and thus regulates prices.

When a contract is agreed with a consumer, some delivery quantities will usually be specified such as Daily contract quantity (DCQ) The daily production which will be supplied; usually averaged over a period such as a quarter year.

Swing factor the amount by which the supply must exceed the DCQ if the customer so requests (e.g. 1.4_DCQ).

Take or pay agreement If the buyer chooses not to accept a specified quantity, he will pay the supplier anyway.

Penalty clause the penalty which the supplier will pay if he fails to deliver the quantity specified within the DCQ and swing factor agreements. The Figure shows the relationship between DCQ and the swing factor. If, for example a swing factor of 1.4 is agreed, then on any one day the customer may

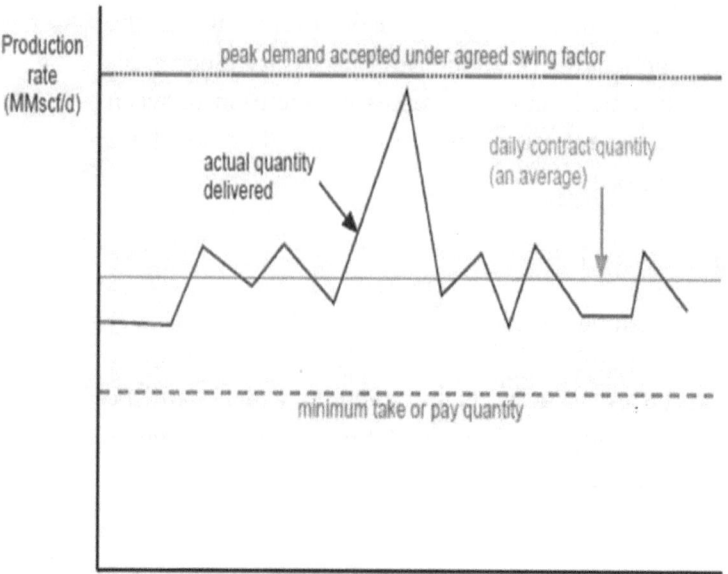

request the producer to provide 1.4 times the DCQ. This means that the producer has to be confident that there is sufficient well potential and transport capacity to meet this demand, otherwise a penalty will be incurred. For most of the time this means that the producer is providing a production potential (sometimes called deliverability) which is not being realized. As compensation to the producer for investing in additional capital to provide this level of redundancy, a higher gas price would be expected. [1]

---

[1] Frank Jahn, Mark Cook and Mark Graham: HYDROCARBON EXPLORATION AND PRODUCTION. 2ND EDITION. Elsevier B.V. 2008. P

3.5. Shale gas production

Natural gas is present in some organic-rich mud rocks. Shale gas has been produced in small quantities for well over a century but recent advances in technology allow much higher rates of production. Shale beds are relatively thin and vertical wells provide access to a very limited volume of rock. It is now possible to drill at any angle and to deviate wells at depth to follow individual shale beds over great distances, allowing access to large volumes of gas-bearing shale.

While production used to be primarily from naturally fractured shales, much recent production from shales is aided by hydraulic fracturing technologies. The fractures provide avenues for gas migration toward the wells.

The new technologies for shale gas production have revolutionized US gas production. Shale gas production was approximately 1% of total US production in 2000 but had risen to 14% of total production in 2009 and is forecast to be 45% of production by 2035. The potential of shale gas has been questioned by some. production is from sweet

212: 214

spots whose nature and lateral extent remains to be better defined. The dramatic rise in US production has, however, spurred interest in shale gas in many other parts of the world, especially in Canada, Central Europe, China, India, and Australia. [1]

Technical improvements in the extraction of hydrocarbons have made it possible and profitable to extract resources trapped in shale formations, triggering what is known as the US shale revolution. Shale gas (SG) and light tight oil (LTO), that is, natural gas and oil confined in the pores of solid and impermeable rocks—shales— are the major products of this revolution.

Hydraulic fracturing and horizontal drilling, although known since the fifties, have been combined with advanced seismological techniques and popularized as "fracking". This process consists of an initial stage of vertical drilling, followed by horizontal drilling, which occurs, according to the characteristics of the field, between 1.5 and 3 km below the surface. Injections of highly pressured liquids (90 % water, 9.5 % sand, ceramic grains and other chemical components) crumble the rocks and free SG and LTO (which we subsequently refer

[1]Ripudaman Malhotra: Fossil Energy. Springer Science+Business Media New York 2013. P 17

to as Shale Fuels— SFs), which are then channeled to the surface. [1]

Production of shale gas started in the 1920s in Ohio, USA using vertical drilled wells. Shale has low matrix permeability, so gas production in commercial quantities requires fractures to provide permeability. The natural fractures are predominantly vertical, so a large number of wells had to be drilled to drain a reservoir. For many years gas production from shales were considered unprofitable. But in the 1980s two new technologies emerged which revolutionized shale gas production—*horizontal drilling* and *hydraulic fracturing*. Horizontal wells reaching as far as 3,000 m create a maximum borehole surface area in contact with the shale. This makes it possible to produce below cultivated land and even underneath cities. A few vertical wells may be the starting point for a large number of horizontal production wells.

Hydraulic fracturing (fracking) is the main difference when producing gas from shale and from a conventional gas reservoir. A liquid at high hydraulic pressure is pumped into the formation which results in fracturing of rock,

---

[1] Rossella Bardazzi • Maria Grazia Pazienza Alberto Tonini: European Energy and Climate Security. Springer International Publishing Switzerland 2016. P 133: 134

usually in the direction normal to the least stress in the formation. At large depth, the cracks have a tendency to become vertical and the influence of the hydraulic cracking may propagate several hundred meters. The fracturing strategy can be tailored for each specific shale formation by numerical simulations based on the special geometry and lithology of the petroleum bearing strata. This opens for large volumes of shale gas to flow to the wellbore and to be produced to the surface.

In an *unconstrained* world, the economics of shale gas is attractive. It currently costs between 2 to 6 Euro to produce one MMBtu of shale gas. This compares well to the production cost of one MMBtu of traditional gas, which amounts to between 0.1 and 6 Euro (IEA 2013b). The word *unconstrained* in the sentence above is important as most of the shale gas is so far produced in the United States and in Canada. With attractive economics, shale gas has been developed rapidly, especially in the US and the supply in natural gas increased drastically. In 2013, the US do not have the possibility to export its natural gas and prices have started to diverge from the price of natural gas in other markets limiting the margins of shale gas producers in the US.

Shale gas reserves are large, at least 210 trillion cubic meters, or enough to satisfy the world current demand for natural gas for another 60 years.

Hydraulic fracturing has raised environmental concerns about ground water contamination, risks to air quality, migration of gases and hydraulic fracturing chemicals leaking to the surface, mishandling of waste, and the health effects of all these, as well as its contribution to raised atmospheric CO_2 levels by enabling the extraction of previously sequestered hydrocarbons. In a recent report (posted to the web in November 2010) by the U. S. Environmental Protection Agency (EPA) on emission factors for greenhouse gas emissions by the oil and gas industry, EPA concluded that shale gas emits larger amounts of methane, a potent greenhouse gas, than does conventional gas, but still far less than coal. [1]

shale gas, requires the use of fracking techniques to exploit gas reserves that were otherwise not viable. This has greatly changed the dynamics of the market, especially in North America where conventional output was in significant decline. This new unconventional

---

[1] Patrick A. Narbel ·Jan Petter Hansen Jan R. Lien: Energy Technologies and Economics. Springer International Publishing Switzerland 2014. P 111: 113

supply has caused a glut in North America due to government restrictions on exports. The resulting substantial fall in North American natural gas prices has led to its greater use in the production of electricity, displacing coal. However, this may not be a tenable situation in the medium term as many current shale gas wells are unprofitable at anywhere near the current price. Shale gas wells also have very high rates of production decline over time, much higher than for conventional gas; greatly reducing the likelihood of production paying back the US$ 10 million that such wells cost. One researcher has estimated that the break-even cost for shale gas is around US$ 9 per million British Thermal Units, rather than the current US$ 3.50 Further complicating the situation may be supply constraints as the profitable finds may be limited to relatively small sweet spots within an overall gas field. For shale gas estimates for EROI vary greatly, from as low as 5:1 to as high as 70:1 and above. This may reflect differences in how EROI was calculated for what is a relatively new resource, and the possibility of "sweet spots" where well productivity is much higher. On the plus side, natural gas does have a reputation for being more climate friendly than coal, with lower amounts of carbon dioxide being released when burnt. However, studies showing that significant amounts of methane can leak from the drilling and transportation processes have undercut this advantage. While methane only stays in the atmosphere for about 14 years, for each of those years it can have a climate changing impact of up to one hundred times that of carbon dioxide. [1]

The term "shale gas" presents a new technique of extracting the natural gas trapped in a certain formation of rocks, which is not possible to exploit with conventional methods. Due to the new production method, the gas produced is also referred to as "unconventional gas." This new exploration and production method requires a more advanced technology than the conventional ways of production. Unconventional gas production entails high-pressure water spraying with chemicals into the cracks in the rock formation to produce a "fracture." Fracturing or hydraulic fracking method allows the producer to access the natural gas trapped in the formation, which would be impossible to access otherwise. The cost is also higher compared to the conventional method. [2]

Unconventional natural gas production has been developed and successfully implemented in the USA in the last decade.

[1] Roger Boyd: Energy and the Financial System Springer Cham Heidelberg New York Dordrecht London 2013. P 18
[2] Ali Nezihi Bilge • Ayhan Özgür Toy Mehmet Erdem Günay: Energy Systems and Management. Springer International Publishing Switzerland 2015. P 91

Once a large natural gas importer, the USA rapidly turned itself into a self-sustaining gas producer, with anticipation of being an exporter in coming years. Many gas importer countries around the world have taken the USA as example and have developed an expectation for duplicating the same experience in their respective gas markets to eliminate the challenges of being gas importer. Turkey is one of the countries where wishful thinking and reality collide and not necessarily coincide.

Accessing shale gas has a list of requirements and environmental risks, which are widely criticized in countries where production has already started. Majority of these challenges are directly applicable in Turkey. Since Turkey is still in the exploratory phase in shale gas development, it is in best interest of Turkey to consider these issues early in the process and take necessary measures to tackle these challenges. 92

The first and the foremost requirement for Turkey to turn itself into a gas sufficient country is the physical existence of substantial amount of recoverable shale gas.

Only existing data on the magnitude of potential shale gas reserves in Turkey belong to American Energy Information Agency (EIA).

According to EIA, Turkey has two promising basins with a total reserve of approximately 450 bcm of natural gas recoverable with unconventional methods. In the EIA analysis, two regions, Thrace and Dadaslar basin in South East Turkey, are marked as two regions with potential. Although some unanimous experts are referred to in media for stating 13 tcm of total gas reserves in Turkey, these figures remain untested and speculative.

Other than data provided by EIA, size of shale gas reserves located in Turkey is not known. TPAO has been active in exploring the regions referred to in the EIA report and confirmed findings on potential rock formations. TPAO has engaged in cooperation with international oil companies that consider the above-mentioned two basins attractive. First agreement is signed in 2010 with Transatlantic and Valeura for exploratory studies in both Thrace region and South East Turkey in the form of a memorandum of understanding. Following this protocol, TPAO entered into another agreement with Shell for cooperation in 2011 and exploratory work started in South East Turkey, close to Diyarbakır province.

TPAO has been historically cautious for not revealing any certain figures on the size of the basins which are worked on. International companies which TPAO works with have also been refraining from publishing figures on how much of a gas reserve they have been estimating on the reserves they engage in. [1]

In the world's drive to access affordable and secure supplies of natural gas, the pursuit of unconventional gas has become inevitable. The International Energy Agency (IEA) estimated in their 2014 New Policies Scenario, that by 2040, unconventional gas could amount to 60% of all added supplies of natural gas in the period and 30% of total natural gas consumption.

Significant progress has been made in Australia where CBM is fuelling several export projects on the East Coast. In China, 2014 targets from the Ministry of Land and Resources (MLR) indicate shale gas and CBM could grow to reflect at least 50% of domestic natural gas production by 2030.17 Saudi Arabia has also made notable progress and is likely to become a commercial shale gas producer before 2020. Argentina's ventures into tight oil are also advancing at a notable pace. In addition, many other NOCs around the world are exploring the potential of their shale gas resources. [2]

---

[1]Ali Nezihi Bilge • Ayhan Özgür Toy Mehmet Erdem Günay: Energy Systems and Management. Springer International Publishing Switzerland 2015. P 94

Shale gas extraction has become a controversial and very competitive resource in the energy mix worldwide. The United States of America (USA) is now advanced on commercial production and already reaping large economic benefits which inter alia includes the expansion of natural gas plant liquids (NGPL), manufacturing chemical, primary metals and replacing the petroleum- based naphtha7 feedstocks with increased use of NGPL feedstocks.

In 2013, an estimation of 885 trillion cubic feet (tcf) of shale gas could be recovered in Europe, representing about 12 % of worldwide shale gas potential from all European countries by the end of 2012. Fourteen European countries are believed to have shale gas resources present in their territories of which largest resources are found in France and Poland. Other states such as Norway, Ukraine, Sweden, Denmark and the United Kingdom (UK) have also large deposits. The EU is the largest world regional market for gas demand estimated at 550 billion cubic meters (BCM) in 2010, which is on the increase whilst production is decreasing in the region. Unconventional gas production in the EU is expected to grow at a much slower rate from 10 BCM in 2010 and

---

[2] World Energy Resources. World Energy Council. 2016. P 15

expected to grow much quicker to 80 BCM by 2035. [1]

3.5.1. Issues surrounding shale gas extraction

Shale gas exploration and production has got technical and environmental issues that has to be seriously looked into for a shale gas project to take off. It is a unique and requires very technical procedure which need a lot of expertise and done in a way that is environmental friendly. Some of them cannot be avoided with the technology and scientific knowledge currently existing and the risks to the environmental and health can happen if the process of extraction is not properly managed. [2]

The production of SG cycle takes five stages starting from identifying the suitable site and preparation, thereby triggering potential environmental and health issues. The first stage involves levelling and clearing the required area

---

[1] Joseph Tawonezvi: The legal and regulatory framework for the EU' shale gas exploration and production regulating public health and environmental impacts. Energ. Ecol. Environ. 2017. P 2

[2] Joseph Tawonezvi: The legal and regulatory framework for the EU' shale gas exploration and production regulating public health and environmental impacts. Energ. Ecol. Environ. 2017. P 5

of land for the well site. There will be transportation of heavy equipment to the site and construction of storage facilities.

The second stage will involve well designing, drilling, cementing and perforation of a hole on the surface and laying pipes, cementing and constructing the wellhead.

The third stage is the technical hydraulic fracturing, by pumping highly pressurized water mixed with sand or other propane and chemicals. Then the well reaches a completion stage where water produced and flowback has to be managed by the operator. Production will then commence and after the well has reached its end it will then need to be decommissioned.

However, all these stages have their peculiar environmental impacts that can start at each stage or can be accumulative from start to finish or through multiple well projects. It is the objective of the EU that individual states are obliged to make laws that regulates the potential environmental impacts on shale gas on all projects they authorize to operate in their States.

There are technical rules and regulations that operators are obliged to comply with throughout the shale gas production processes. The MS through their competent authorities are compelled to monitor the activities of the licenses in their jurisdictions and to make sure they are complying with the minimum standards expected in these types of projects. [1]

3.5.2. Global Perspective of Shale Gas Production

It is projected that by 2035 the global energy consumption increases by 37 % from today's levels with India and China accounting for half of the growth according to BP (2015). In order to give a broad view about hydrocarbon fuels, in 2014, 80.6 % of the total primary energy supply was based on fossil fuels such as oil, natural gas and coal. In 2014, the annual production of natural gas was 3,524 bcm (OECD/IEA 2015). [2]

---

[1] Joseph Tawonezvi: The legal and regulatory framework for the EU' shale gas exploration and production regulating public health and environmental impacts. Energ. Ecol. Environ. 2017. P 5

[2] Georgios M. Kopanos · Pei Liu Michael C. Georgiadis: Advances in Energy Systems Engineering. Springer International Publishing Switzerland 2017. P 5

In recent decades, large-scale production of shale gas has been considered as a major issue in the U.S. energy industry. In accordance with its great economic potential and environmental concerns, shale gas process and supply chain optimization has become one of the most popular research areas. In this chapter, we provide a comprehensive overview of the supply chain management and process design problems in shale gas industry. We summarize four major research challenge areas, namely the design and planning of shale gas supply chain, water management in hydraulic fracturing, sustainability concerns in shale gas industry, and design and optimization in shale gas processing system.

Shale gas is known as unconventional natural gas extracted from shale rock layer and has emerged as one of the most promising energy sources within the last few decades. With the discovery of huge shale gas reserves all over the world, a "shale revolution" starts in the U.S. and keeps spreading out in other countries. In 2005, the U.S. barely produces any natural gas from shale formations. Nowadays, nearly 44 % of the total natural gas withdrawal is from shale gas wells. [1]

---

[1]Georgios M. Kopanos · Pei Liu Michael C. Georgiadis: Advances in Energy Systems Engineering. Springer International Publishing Switzerland 2017. P 21

According to the Annual Energy Outlook 2015 by the U.S. Energy Information Administration (EIA 2015), natural gas production is expected to grow by an average rate of 1.6 % per year from 2012 to 2040. As a result, the percentage of the U.S. total natural gas production from shale gas is expected to increase to 53 % by 2040.

The remarkable development of large-scale shale gas production would not be possible without the hydraulic fracturing and horizontal drilling technologies. Different from the conventional natural gas, shale gas is embedded in the shale rocks that can be a few thousand feet deep. Therefore, special techniques are required to withdraw this unconventional resource. By using hydraulic fracturing, millions of gallons of fracturing fluid (about 90 % water, 9.5 % sand, and 0.5 % chemical additives) is pumped underground under high pressure (up to 70 Mpa), fracturing the rock layer and holding fractures open, thus forcing the shale gas and/or oil to flow back to the surface. The horizontal drilling, on the other hand, is a drilling process in which the well is turned horizontally at depth. Compared with the vertical drilling, horizontal drilling allows us to drill multiple wells at a single shale site/pad. As a result, a horizontal well site is able to produce more energy with fewer wellbores, which significantly reduces the capital investment and improves the efficiency for shale gas production. [1]

Shale gas production of a single well normally features a high initial production rate followed by an astounding decline from 60 to 90 % after the first three years. This characteristic is mainly caused by the pressure depletion and inherently low permeability of the reservoir. Consequently, operators need to regularly drill new wells to maintain a stable production profile, which results in a scheduling problem. Additionally, based on the composition, shale gas can be classified as dry gas and wet gas, and the key difference is the content of natural gas liquids (NGLs). The NGLs are defined as light hydrocarbons including ethane, propane, butane and heavier components, which typically have substantially higher market values than methane gas. Dry gas is almost pure methane with trace NGLs. Although methane is still the dominant component in wet gas, the amount of NGLs is significant enough to require further processing. Depending on the location, both the estimated ultimate recovery (EUR) and shale gas composition of a shale well may have significant variance. All of these issues render the optimal

---

[1]Georgios M. Kopanos · Pei Liu Michael C. Georgiadis: Advances in Energy Systems Engineering. Springer International Publishing Switzerland 2017. P 22

design and operation in the shale gas industry a challenging topic. [1]

The shale gas produced at shale site is generally considered as raw shale gas that needs further processing. The processing service is typically provided by midstream processors. Through the shale gas processing, impurities such as compounds and gases, oil, and water mixed with the natural gas are removed. Two major products, "pipeline-quality" sales gas and NGLs, are extracted and sold separately. The sales gas is normally delivered to major intrastate and interstate pipeline transmission systems and further sent to final customers. The NGLs, on the other hand, can be used as feedstock for the production of value-added chemicals, such as olefins and gasoline blending stocks. With the rapid development of shale gas industry, excessive supply of NGLs requires more cost-effective shale gas processing designs and conversion alternatives for a better use of this valuable byproduct. [2]

Despite the great economic potential stimulated by the shale gas, one major concern

---

[1]Georgios M. Kopanos · Pei Liu Michael C. Georgiadis: Advances in Energy Systems Engineering. Springer International Publishing Switzerland 2017. P 22
[2]Georgios M. Kopanos · Pei Liu Michael C. Georgiadis: Advances in Energy Systems Engineering. Springer International Publishing Switzerland 2017. P 23

impeding the expansion of shale gas industry is its negative impact on the climate change. Methane is about 25 times more potent greenhouse gas (GHG) than carbon dioxide based on the 100-year global warming potential (GWP). A small amount of methane leakage could lead to enormous greenhouse gas footprint. Additionally, supply chain activities such as shale gas production, processing, transportation, and gas-based power generation could incur large amount of GHG emissions as well. There have been extensive studies published evaluating the life cycle carbon footprint of shale gas. However, the shortage of decision-support tools and methodologies still exists, which requires the development of corresponding optimization models for more sustainable design alternatives in the shale gas industry. [1]

3.5.3. Optimization Models for Shale Gas Supply Chain

Conventional natural gas supply chain has been fully studied in the literature. A variety of models have been proposed addressing the design and planning problems in oil/gas supply

---

[1] Georgios M. Kopanos · Pei Liu Michael C. Georgiadis: Advances in Energy Systems Engineering. Springer International Publishing Switzerland 2017. P 23

chains. In recent decades, with the rapid development of shale gas industry, many research studies arise specifically focusing on the optimization of shale gas system. Knudsen and Foss (2013) present a novel operational scheme for enhanced utilization of late-life shale gas systems. In this work, a large number of geographically distributed wells and pads are considered, which are producing at low erratic rates due to reservoir pressure depletion and well liquid loading. By using a shale-gas well and reservoir proxy model, a generalized disjunctive program (GDP) is formulated. The proposed cyclic shut-in and production strategy is expected to avoid well liquid loading and improve the overall production. Following this work, Knudsen et al. (2014) propose a Lagrangian relaxation-based decomposition scheme for solving large field-wide well scheduling problems in shale gas systems. Furthermore, they explore the integration of shale gas supply with local natural-gas power generation. A large-scale mixed-integer linear program (MILP) is proposed, and the results indicate a potential increase of profit for shale gas operators by improving well Scheduling. [1]

some new developments are presented. First, a novel superstructure for shale gas

---

[1] Georgios M. Kopanos · Pei Liu Michael C. Georgiadis: Advances in Energy Systems Engineering. Springer International Publishing Switzerland 2017. P 26

development problem is proposed, which captures the distinctive "tree"-structure of typical shale gas gathering system. Different delivery options including processing sales routes and direct delivery sales arcs are explicitly distinguished. In addition, discrete sizes of pipeline diameters and compressors are considered. Thus, the corresponding capacity constraints are captured by mixed-integer linear constraints, and the economies of scale is taken into account without involving concave cost functions. Moreover, this work extends the scope of shale gas development problem to include strategic decisions, such as the selection of delivery nodes, arrangement of delivery agreements, and procurement of delivery capacity. Most importantly, the spatial composition variations of shale gas are explicitly addressed in this work. The quality of shale gas is required to satisfy the delivery specifications at delivery nodes. Besides, depending on the price forecast, the upstream operator will target different shale gas qualities. The resulting problem is a large-scale, nonconvex, MINLP problem with an objective to maximize the NPV over the planning horizon. Based on the results, the shale gas development is proven to be quality sensitive. Additionally, the profitability of shale gas development projects can be improved by a few million U.S. dollars through the optimization of return-to-pad operations, equipment utilization, and strategic delivery agreements. [1]

3.5.4. Shale Gas Supply Chain

During the last decade, the production of shale gas has progressively increased in importance in the energy sector, the economy of the United States, and more recently in the global economy. There is a strong indication that shale gas resources are and will continue to play an important role in the global energy market in the next decades. [2]

Shale gas refers to natural gas trapped within sedimentary rocks formed by laminar deposits of fine-grained clay particles and organic matter. Geological processes of burial and compaction through continuous sedimentation on top provide the necessary temperature and pressure conditions to initiate the thermogenic breakdown of the organic matter to generate oil and gas. Shale formations are characterized by extremely low matrix permeability, between 10−6 and 10−2 millidarcy

---

[1] Georgios M. Kopanos · Pei Liu Michael C. Georgiadis: Advances in Energy Systems Engineering. Springer International Publishing Switzerland 2017. P 28: 29

[2] Georgios M. Kopanos · Pei Liu Michael C. Georgiadis: Advances in Energy Systems Engineering. Springer International Publishing Switzerland 2017. P 49

(md) versus 100–10,000 md in conventional oil and gas reservoirs. Due to the low permeability, any migration processes of fossil resources towards upper formations are significant only over geologic time, i.e. millions of years. This has important repercussions from an industrial viewpoint. For example, the exploration stage is comparatively easier than in conventional reservoirs, however, the production stage is quite challenging. The exploitation of shale resources is highly dependent on artificial stimulation techniques, such as the hydraulic fracturing, which are used to increase the connectivity within the shale matrix, facilitating the flow of natural gas from the formation matrix to the well. Recent advances in horizontal well drilling and hydraulic fracturing technologies have made the development of shale gas reservoirs economically attractive. Nonetheless, the low matrix permeability limits the drainage area of the well mostly to the extent of the rock formation stimulated by the hydraulic fracturing. This results in recovery factors in the order of 20–30 % which are markedly lower than those for conventional natural gas resources, commonly between 80 and 90 %. Due to low recovery factors, companies involved in the exploitation of these resources opt for the implementation of intensive drilling schemes to benefit from economy of scales. Consequently, the feasibility and profitability of a shale gas reservoir are strongly determined by production costs and productivity, hence, minor changes in the market conditions can have substantial repercussions on the development of these resources. Moreover, a sustainable shale gas production is an essential aspect that can be handled through collaboration between policy makers, industry sector as well as engagement of neighboring communities. In particular, the depletion and degradation of water sources, as well as the potential for underground water contamination, are major drawbacks that could and do hinder the development of these resources. [1]

---

[1]Georgios M. Kopanos · Pei Liu Michael C. Georgiadis: Advances in Energy Systems Engineering. Springer International Publishing Switzerland 2017. P 50

4. Unconventional Oil and Gas

Given the potentially significant contribution that unconventional oil and gas may have in Europe, it is important to include these sources in the supply cost curves.

Unconventional oil quantities—composed of heavy oil, oil sands, and shale oil—are taken from the GEA (2012). Although unconventional oil is more abundant than the conventional on a global scale, it is relatively scarce in Europe—where heavy oil is the largest (3.2 BBOE), followed closely by shale oil (2.3 BBOE) and oil sands (1.0 BBOE). The total is approximately 6.5 BBOE, which pales in comparison to the conventional oil endowment estimated in the previous section at about 208 BBOE. By contrast, the unconventional gas endowment—composed of coalbed methane (CBM), tight gas, and shale gas—is vast and has the potential to contribute to European demand if regulatory and environmental hurdles can be overcome. Shale gas is the most abundant (1,251 TCF), followed by CBM (833 TCF) and tight gas (416 TCF). The total, approximately 2,500 TCF (GEA 2012), is somewhat larger than the conventional gas endowment estimated in the previous section at about 2,188 TCF. [1]

---

[1] Walter Leal Filho • Vlasios Voudouris: Global Energy

In the last few decades, Argentina has been facing an energy shortage that is very difficult to balance in the medium term by means of an increase in the production of nuclear and hydroelectric power, of renewable resources, coal—which is practically irrelevant—oil, and gas.

The results of unconventional oil and gas exploitation in the USA, which were exponentially positive in the short term, started a worldwide trend in that direction, including Argentina, where in the last decade the reserves, and oil and gas production decreased, despite the increase in active wells and in the water/oil ratio.

Unconventional sources of tight and shale gas/oil have been proven to exist here, combined with a profound geological knowledge—as these source rocks were drilled and tested during conventional oil and gas exploitation—and with generally available installed infrastructure. After the Neuquén Basin, which is the most favourable basin and currently in production, the San Jorge Gulf Basin has very good prospects of success in shale gas/oil exploitation.

Policy and Security. Springer-Verlag London 2013. P 146

The source formations are Pozo D-129, the main source rock in the basin—within which it is widely distributed—Pozo Anticlinal Aguada Bandera, and Pozo Cerro Guadal, the last two recognized as a whole as Neocomian and as being the oldest in the region. Unlike the case of the Neuquén Basin, exploitation is incipient.

The most favorable general conditions for the future, besides the lithology and thicknesses, are the good information available, collected from the historical exploration in the area, and the presence of certain basic infrastructure (e.g. access roads, batteries, pipelines, electric power). Among the negative conditions are the limited availability of water and the restrictive use regulations.

The water requirements are greater than those of conventional oil and gas production, of the order of 7500–30,000 m3 per well for fracking, which would constitute 70% of the water total, with the remaining 30% being used in the drilling.

There are cases in which up to 174,000 m3 were required for a six-well platform. Even though the amounts are not excessive, they are significant demands for an arid region.

The availability of water resources is considerably lower than in the Neuquén Basin, where surface sources (Neuquén River, and the Mari Menuco and Los Barreales dams)—which are amply sufficient for large-scale supply—can be used.

On the other hand, in the San Jorge Gulf Basin, the surface resources are practically limited to the Senguerr River—from whose underflow until not long-ago water was collected—since the Deseado River is an intermittent stream and the Chico River has been cut off. The Musters and Colhué Huapi lakes, in turn, are highly compromised at present, due to the progressive decrease in contributions.

Consequently, groundwater is essential within the framework of comprehensive management. In the SGS, the Patagonian and Santa Cruz aquifers are bound by use restrictions, and in the Province of Chubut the guidelines may be issued by the enforcement authority. Water in the SGI aquifers is brackish.

Even though in unconventional oil and gas resources there are no compatibility problems because source rocks do not act as aquifers, the quality of water in the injection may be an issue due to reactivity; the details are not known for confidentiality reasons. The management proposed includes the brackish water of the SGI, part of the underflow of the Senguerr River, and water recovered from the flowback, which in the Neuquén Basin is of approximately 35% in volume. In general, percentages between 20 and 70% are mentioned, so the most convenient water mixture must be carried out in each case, taking into consideration the logistical factor regarding transportation and temporary storage. [1]

Of the unconventional sources of oil, recovery from tar sands is being expanded rapidly. A tar sand is essentially a dead oil field. When erosion brings an oil field to the surface, the smaller molecules evaporate, and a nearly solid tar is left in the reservoir rock. Although tar sands exist around the world, Alberta contains two enormous tar sand deposits: Athabaska and Cold Lake. Tarry oil is extracted by mining the sand, contacting it with hot water, and separating the oil. To tell the truth, the oil isn't all that great; it contains a lot of sulfur. The original tar sand recovery plant, opened in 1978, was profitable in the sense that oil sales paid the operating costs, but the plant took forever to pay back the capital investment.12 Improved methods followed; as of 1999, 2 billion dollars is

---

([1])Mario Alberto Hernández Nilda González • Lisandro Hernández: Hydrogeology of a Large Oil-and-Gas Basin in Central Patagonia. 2017. P 74: 75

being invested in new tar sand operations in Alberta. Closely related to tar sands are reservoir rocks filled with "heavy" oil, oil that is too viscous to move using ordinary production practices.

If a tar sand is a moribund oil field, an oil shale is an unborn oil field. An "oil shale" contains neither oil nor shale; it is an ordinary petroleum source rock that has never been buried into the oil window. A particularly large oil shale deposit exists where Utah, Colorado, and Wyoming come together. As the first transcontinental railroad reached the town of Green River, Wyoming, a work crew gathered up a circle of rocks to surround their campfire. The rocks caught fire. They were not coal; the heat from the campfire caused thermal cracking to produce oil, and it was the oil that was burning. The rock unit, the source rock, was eventually named the Green River Formation. After the formation was deposited, mountain ranges arose that broke the original lake basin into several pieces. The Wyoming portion is the Green River Basin, in Utah it is the Uinta Basin, and in Colorado it is the Piceance Basin. ("Piceance" is a local name, made to look French again by early map makers. The word is pronounced "piss ants.") In the western Uinta Basin, some of the source rocks have been buried into the oil window; two midsize oil fields produce oil whose source is the Green River Formation.

The Green River Formation turned out to be unusual in several ways. It was not marine; it was formed in a saline lake. Almost half of the world's supply of sodium carbonate is mined from the Green River Formation. Unique minerals occur in the Green River Formation.

Spectacular fossils occur because no scavengers could live on the oxygen-free lake bottom. And, for our purposes, the oil that could be released from the Green River oil shale is roughly equal to all the world's conventional oil. [1]

---

[1] K E N N E T H S . D E F F E Y E S: Hubbert's Peak. Princeton University Press. 2001. P 168: 169

5. OPEC

This organization is composed of 11 countries: Algeria, Indonesia, Iran, Iraq, Kuwait, Libya, Nigeria, Qatar, Saudi Arabia, the United Arab Emirates, and Venezuela. OPEC's member countries hold about two-thirds of the world's proven oil reserves (about 900 billion barrels) and supply about 40% of the world's oil production (about 50% of total exports). The objective of OPEC is to stabilize the international price range for crude oil by controlling the amount of crude oil sold in worldwide markets. Because the price of light, sweet crude oil is currently much higher than their previous target of $25 to $30 per barrel, it is clear that the demand is close to the maximum production capacity of both OPEC and petroleum-exporting countries not part of OPEC. Of course, this high price and high production rate maximizes the income of the petroleum-exporting countries as long as the petroleum-importing countries can maintain healthy economies.

Thus, despite the high cost of crude oil, OPEC has less influence on the crude price than it did previously. Of course, if OPEC were to decide to cut production, the price would greatly increase. However, with all the OPEC countries producing at maximum capacity with the exception of Iraq and Saudi Arabia, there is not much OPEC can do to lower the price. Because the consumer pays the price of petroleum products, not crude oil, a shortage of refinery capacity can also raise the price consumers pay as well as local taxes. To combat the effect of a refining shortage, OPEC countries, particularly Saudi Arabia, have made plans to add refining capacity of 5.9 million barrels per day by 2012 and export refinery products.

The influence of OPEC also has been reduced by the increase in the amount of petroleum exported by countries not part of OPEC, particularly Russia and Norway (the latter only the seventh largest producer in the world), which are the second and third largest exporters of petroleum, respectively.

Iraq with 115 billion barrels has the third largest reserves of conventional oil to that of Saudi Arabia, 267 billion barrels, and Iran, 132 billion barrels.

However, Iraq only ranks 14th in amount of oil produced. This is because of the United Nations sanctions placed on Iraq after the 1991 Persian Gulf War, initiated by Iraq's invasion of Kuwait. More recently, Iraq's production is even less because of the obstruction by those in Iraq opposed to the occupation of the United States and Great Britain and to the present Iraq government. The facilities and equipment for the production and transport of petroleum are also much below standard in Iraq, but do not warrant upgrading until the threat of obstruction is mitigated.

Obviously, if Iraq were to achieve full production, the petroleum price would greatly drop unless the rest of OPEC would cut their production accordingly. At this writing, the unrest in Nigeria, an OPEC member, also threatens to reduce production in the eighth largest exporter of petroleum. [1]

5.1. OPEC AND THE UNITED STATES

The price of oil had been on an upward trend for over a decade, with the exception of a temporary price collapse in 2008. Th at changed in 2014 when oil from American fracking created a surplus on the market and OPEC did not reduce its output to buoy the price. The move demonstrated the extent of influence OPEC has over the price of oil. OPEC itself

---

[1]Irwin A. Wiehe: Process Chemistry of Petroleum Macromolecules. Taylor & Francis Group, LLC. 2008. P 3:4

cannot set the price of oil. It had wrested control of the posted price from the international oil companies over the 1960s by demanding it have a say over that price. In the 1970s, it was able to set the price for its oil, which set a benchmark for what companies then charged for oil from other regions from where they extracted oil. Once futures trading in oil was introduced, however, OPEC was unable to simply set a price itself anymore, and reluctantly had to accept that the market would dictate the price of oil. The only mechanism it had at its disposal to influence the price of oil was regulating its output by setting quotas for its members. That had been the concept on which OPEC was based when it was created by the Venezuelan Minister of Hydrocarbons Juan Pablo Perez Alfonso. In reality, however, in its first decade OPEC did not enforce those quotas. It was only when the price of oil collapsed in the early 1980s and futures trading was introduced that the organization began to take those quotas seriously. With most members disregarding their allocated quotas and producing more oil to make up for the low price, thereby driving the price further down, all the while expecting Saudi Arabia as the largest producer to cut its production to keep prices higher, the Middle East kingdom reacted by refusing to curb its output if its fellow OPEC members would not restrict theirs. It reasoned that with its low production costs per barrel, it could still make a profit even if it sold oil for just $2 to refineries and split the profit on the refined product with them. Few other countries could produce oil at such a low cost and the more expensive oil that was being produced would eventually be forced out of the market. Th at gambit eventually paid off and also shocked Saudi Arabia's fellow OPEC members into curbing their errant behavior.

In 2014, it appeared there would be a re-enactment of the 1980s unrestrained production although the reasons behind it were somewhat different.

Just as in the 1980s, new oil from Norway, Mexico, and the Soviet Union was coming on the market creating a surplus and driving the price down, so too by 2014 new oil from American fracking, Russia, Kazakhstan, Brazil, Canada, and the coast of west Africa was making itself felt on the market.

North African and Middle East countries affected by the Arab Spring revolutions a couple of years earlier had recovered and were producing oil at the same levels as before the revolutions. Once again, OPEC members looked to Saudi Arabia and the wealthier members to curb their production to keep the price up, but the Saudis, Kuwaitis, and

Emiratis were unwilling to give up their market share for the benefit of Venezuela and other poorer members.

Within OPEC itself, there is no real mechanism for setting quotas. It is not based on a country's proven reserves, or Venezuela would have the lion's share of the quota. It is also not based on population or on GDP. Production capacity is one of the factors influencing a county's quota, and by 2014, with Venezuela being recognized as the world's largest holder of proven reserves, talks with Iran over its nuclear weapons program intensifying, raising the spectra that sanctions could be lifted against Tehran, making it easier for that country to increase production, and the dropping price leading other OPEC states to want to increase their own production, the three wealthier states realized if they cut their own production they would have a very difficult time getting that share back in the future. Th us, at the November 2014 OPEC meeting in Vienna, they dug in their heels and refused to cut their share. Other OPEC states did not offer to cut back on their own production so OPEC maintained its level of production from the previous year. As OPEC was producing approximately 40% of the world's oil, any decision to cut or increase production would have an impact on global supplies. Once the word came out that OPEC was not going to cut production, the price of oil began falling. At the same time, a number of rigs in the USA stopped pumping because they could not produce oil profitably if the price fell below $60. Projects to develop Venezuela's extra heavy oil were also put on hold, and there were questions as to whether Brazil's Lula field could produce at a profit if oil were in the $50s range, as well as fields in the Gulf of Mexico. Despite the drop in the price of oil, OPEC's wealthier members held firm in the succeeding biannual meetings and continued to maintain their production. Kuwait was believed to be best placed to weather the low oil price for several years, but the Saudis also reportedly could still meet their annual budget for four years owing to their sovereign wealth fund, currency reserves, and other assets. It was even reported that they were looking at trimming their budget so they could continue running with oil priced at $50 a barrel for eight years. [1]

Free world oil production is on the rise again after the 1974-1975 slowdown in response to the quadrupling of energy prices and a world-wide recession. Free world oil production is currently approaching 53 million barrels per day, of which more than 60 percent is supplied by

[1]Thijs Van de Graaf • Benjamin K. Sovacool Arunabha Ghosh • Florian Kern • Michael T. Klare: The Palgrave Handbook of the International Political Economy of Energy. 2016. P 233: 255

OPEC countries. Non-cartel countries' oil production is also expanding briskly - perhaps by 9-10 percent per annum. In spite of the new discoveries, induding those in Alaska, North Africa, Mexico, and the North Sea, these additional sources will only add six years of life to the world's present requirements.

Canada, despite reduced exports to the United States, is still dependent upon OPEC oil imports to the extent of about 480 thousand barrels per day, or about 75 percent of our total oil imports. Canada is thus still in a very vulnerable position vis-a-vis the future security of oil imports from abroad should political disruptions, another Middle East war, etc., reduce or cut off these important energy sources.
(1)

Middle East producers are still very much in the driver's seat - aided by the Americans who seem unwilling to force conservation measures that would tend to weaken oil prices. But OPEC members are also facing considerable problems in determining a pricing structure for crude oil exports. Assuming that economic rather than political

---

([1])w. T. Ziemba S. L. Schwartz: ENERGY POLICY MODELING: UNITED STATES AND CANADIAN EXPERIENCES Volume II. Martinus Nijhoff Publishing, Boston 1st edition 1980. P 338

considerations will determine future pricing policies, some of the factors that will affect future pricing are: [1]

1. OPEC must take account of its existing reserves and their impact on future revenues in determining prices. Saudi Arabia, and the Emirates have the bulk of these reserves and are using their leverage to exert a moderating influence.

2. Other OPEC countries do not have extensive reserves and are spending

their oil revenues rapidly. Their objective is to increase oil prices as quickly as possible to pay for imports and rapidly growing debt charges.

3. OPEC's share of total free world production is 63 percent and declining. Non-cartel countries respond quickly to changes in price, thereby providing additional production in response to higher prices and/or conservation measures by OPEC.

---

[1] W. T. Ziemba S. L. Schwartz: ENERGY POLICY MODELING: UNITED STATES AND CANADIAN EXPERIENCES Volume II. Martinus Nijhoff Publishing, Boston 1st edition 1980. P 338: 339

4. Non-conventional oil and oil substitutes are rapidly being developed. Higher prices will bring many more of these developments onstream.

The lack of a comprehensive energy policy in the United States has had a significant impact on the U.S. international payments position. The U.S. deficit on energy products, principally crude oil, reached $45 billion in 1977. Until the government deregulates domestic oil and gas prices or imposes a surtax on imports, there will unlikely be any quick turnaround in the U.S. balance of payments and the downward pressure on the U.S. dollar. The proposal to attach a well-head tax to the OPEC-determined world price of crude oil is no solution - that would merely reinforce the OPEC cartel by adding U.S. oil production to world output so that more than 80 percent of the free world's production would be priced by OPEC.

There have been some recent U.S. proposals to deregulate all newly discovered natural gas by 1985. Initially, gas prices would be allowed to climb to $1.93 a thousand cubic feet from $1.49 at present. Then, in 1981, gas prices would escalate roughly in line with the rate of inflation plus 3.7 percent per year. Simply put, real gas prices would be rising until decontrol becomes effective in 1985. If this proposal is enacted, and there are signs that it will be, Canadian gas, which currently is much more expensive than American would be much more competitively priced in the U.S. market. But, the corollary of this could also occur: higher gas prices would mean the development of heretofore uneconomic production of existing natural gas reserves in the United States. We could end up with higher gas prices and no new export markets for Canadian gas. [1]

5.2. OPEC Profits and Their Limit

There are four distinct periods in the early history of OPEC: (1) the formative years, 1960–69; (2) the 1970–74 period of hasty transition; (3) the 1975–80 period of unsettled and slow adjustment to the global change; (4) and the post-1980 adjustment to the globalization of oil.

In the early formative years, OPEC was directly dominated by the IPC. In this period, even though global oil was moving toward the end of its transitional stage, the role of OPEC was passive and the magnitude of its

---

[1] W. T. Ziemba S. L. Schwartz: ENERGY POLICY MODELING: UNITED STATES AND CANADIAN EXPERIENCES Volume II. Martinus Nijhoff Publishing, Boston 1st edition 1980. P 340

oil rent was not even slightly reflective of the existing interregional differential productivities. OPEC members had no control over the production of oil or the conditions of contracts associated with the IPC. In the transitional period of 1970–74, OPEC as a whole was a little schizophrenic, displaying divisions and detachment with respect to absorption and digestion of the enormous change that was speeding through like a runaway train. Aside from the inconsistent political posturing by the member countries, the rapid structural changes that had been long in motion, beneath and against the visible façade of US foreign policy— particularly manifested by the veneer of the Nixon Doctrine in the Persian Gulf—were too much for OPEC to bear in such a short time.

Besides, not all the member countries were on a comparable level of economic development; neither were they on the same level of social and political development. Yet, against all unevenness and incongruity, the share of OPEC's oil rents had skyrocketed in this period, as the significant rise of "posted" prices between October and December 1973 would demonstrate. The necessity of an active role on the part of OPEC, however, cannot simply be elucidated by such an active role itself, without entering the realm of tautology or circular reasoning. These activities are tantamount to both *necessity* and *sufficiency* of the objective forces that led to the unification and production of oil on a modern capitalistic basis. Thus, essentially, the quarrel of OPEC and the IPC ought to be understood in light of the internal contradictions of capitalism on a global scale, and not so much as the skin-deep "nationalistic" outlook of OPEC. [1]

([1])Cyrus Bina: A Prelude to the Foundation of Political Economy. PALGRAVE MACMILLAN. 2013. P 94:95

6. World Petroleum Economics

It is difficult for a technical book to capture the economics of petroleum, which historically has changed widely so frequently. However, worldwide petroleum economics has such a profound influence on the development and application of petroleum technology that it cannot be ignored. Thus, the reader should decide which of the following pertains to the time he or she is reading this section and modify the conclusions accordingly.

In 2007, when the writing of this book was completed, petroleum economics was greatly influenced by Organization of Petroleum Exporting Countries (OPEC); the occupation of Iraq by the United States and Great Britain; the booming, but emerging, economies of China and India; the strong appetite of the United States for petroleum products; the decreasing rate of discovery of sources of light crude oils; the approach to full refining capacity; and the threat that the burning of fossil fuels has begun to cause global warming. Petroleum economics is greatly influenced by the political situation in many countries because there is a delicate balance between supply and demand. A small shortage or surplus in petroleum causes wide swings in its price. However, at the time of the writing of this book, the price of light, sweet crude oil has reached above $90 per barrel, showing a greater danger of shortage than surplus. [1]

6.1. PETROLEUM INDUSTRY INVESTMENT

Consider recent developments related to the petroleum industry which supplies over three quarters of the primary energy needs in Canada. The financing of this sector must be considered in several distinct areas. These include the exploration and development of conventional oil and gas, tar sand and heavy oil plants, and pipeline construction. Each of the three areas of activity involves a substantially different institutional and economic set of considerations which must be faced by potential investors. The financing issues vary accordingly.

The most controversial area of investment and financing in Canada since the oil crisis in 1973 has been the conventional oil and gas industry. With an existing production capability of approximately 0.7 billion barrels of oil and 2,360 billion cubic feet of gas annually, the petroleum industry stood to gain vast

[1]Irwin A. Wiehe: Process Chemistry of Petroleum Macromolecules. Taylor & Francis Group, LLC. 2008. P 3

increases in gross revenues from the advance in price of imported oil from the earlier levels of around $3.00 to $12.00 per barrel. The industry was, of course, spared from this embarrassment of riches as both the provincial and federal governments moved in to claim increased shares of the petroleum dollar. [1]

Control of crude oil and gas prices was imposed by the Federal Government, initially as a simple price freeze. Subsequently, increases in wellhead prices have been made at regular intervals with the announced intent of bringing domestic crude prices to the level of world prices and gas prices to the Btu equivalent parity with oil. As of 1978, domestic crude prices were still approximately 25 percent below world prices. These controls on wellhead prices were accompanied by a tax on crude exported to the United States and a subsidy on oil imports on the East Coast.

Price controls, while having the beneficial effect of reducing the suddenness of price changes for the Canadian consumer and industry, have two unfortunate economic side effects. The first is the reduction of incentives

---

[1] W. T. Ziemba S. L. Schwartz: ENERGY POLICY MODELING: UNITED STATES AND CANADIAN EXPERIENCES Volume II. Martinus Nijhoff Publishing, Boston 1st edition 1980. P 372: 373

for the users of energy to adjust their consumption to reflect the higher replacement cost of oil or gas. Conservation measures such as the purchase of a more gas efficient automobile or the installation of insulation in the home become less urgent while the consumer is shielded from the impact of the new energy environment. Industrial users find modifications of processes or replacement of fuel inefficient equipment harder to justify in terms of immediate cost savings. As in the historic-cost pricing of electricity, demand for the scarce resources continues at levels above that which would result if the full replacement costs were charged. [1]

Of course, price controls are not the only factor inhibiting the economic response of the oil and gas supply industry. The imposition of Provincial royalties and Federal and Provincial taxes have been the main cause of the limited Investment response which we have seen to date. The producing provinces increased the effective royalty rate on existing production from 12 percent prior to the OPEC created crisis, to approximately 34.4 percent. At the same time, the Federal government, in attempting to protect its revenues, made changes rendering royalties

[1] w. T. Ziemba S. L. Schwartz: ENERGY POLICY MODELING: UNITED STATES AND CANADIAN EXPERIENCES Volume II. Martinus Nijhoff Publishing, Boston 1st edition 1980. P 372

non-deductible for tax purposes and embarked on a series of other modifications in the taxation structure. Analysis of the impact of taxation and royalties was provided by Quirin and Kalymon (1977). Without reinvestment, approximately 22.4 percent of gross oil or gas revenues would accrue to the Federal government in taxes and a further 5.6 percent to the Provincial governments. After royalties and taxes, the effective wellhead price would thus be approximately 37.8 percent of the control set price or about $4.54 per barrel if world prices of $12.00 were to prevail. An additional $2.40 per barrel could be generated in tax deferrals if approximately $6.00 of the gross revenue from each barrel produced is reinvested in exploration or development. Somewhat reduced levels of royalty payments on "new" supplies would provide an additional 0.97¢ to the effective wellhead price. In summary, the effective wellhead price which directs the reinvestment process of the private sector is only a fraction of the full opportunity cost of foregone domestic production. [1]

The nature of petroleum exploration and development is such that the industry has historically been unable to obtain debt financing

---

[1] W. T. Ziemba S. L. Schwartz: ENERGY POLICY MODELING: UNITED STATES AND CANADIAN EXPERIENCES Volume II. Martinus Nijhoff Publishing, Boston 1st edition 1980. P 374

at anything but a small percentage of total capitalization. In contrast to the electric utilities, less than 10 percent of capital expenditures have historically been financed through bonds. In 1974, debt constituted approximately 16.6 percent of the permanent funds of oil producing companies. This reflects the market perception of oil and gas as a substantially riskier economic activity than utility investment. On the basis of a comparison with the rates of return allowed on equity investment for regulated utilities in Canada and several alternative risk measures which were applied, I would conclude that a return on total capital employed of approximately 19 percent after-tax would be required to attract capital investment in petroleum exploration and development in Canada today. Such a return should be considered simply as an expectation since actual results which shall be realized in the future are unpredictable. However, the assurance that such levels are unachievable or unacceptable would likely substantially shrink the pool of capital which will be available whether from internally or externally generated funds. In recent years, the government's treatment of the oil industry has taken the semblance of procedures applicable to a regulated utility and full capital costs must be properly recognized if the viability of the industry to operate is not to be impaired. [1]

---

[1] w. T. Ziemba S. L. Schwartz: ENERGY POLICY MODELING: UNITED STATES AND CANADIAN

6.2. Importance and Challenges of Petroleum

Anthropologists have classified periods of ancient history by the important materials of the time, such as the Bronze Age or the Iron Age. However, fuel better classifies modern man because there is no greater dependency of modern technology than on the energy that drives it. If this is the case, then the twentieth century was clearly the Petroleum Age. It has been the fuel of choice for driving our vehicles: automobiles, trucks, airplanes, ships, and trains. In addition, the by-products of producing these fuels provided the petrochemical building blocks of the twentieth century materials: plastics, synthetic fibers, and synthetic elastomers.

Although other forms of energy, such as coal, natural gas, and nuclear energy, have made their bid to overtake petroleum, the liquid state of petroleum gives it a great edge. As a result, it can be easily stored and transported in a concentrated form of chemical energy that is relatively safe. It is no wonder that, in the 1970s, when we thought the supply of petroleum was running out, the consequence was a world

EXPERIENCES Volume II. Martinus Nijhoff Publishing, Boston 1st edition 1980. P 375

economic and political problem, the "energy crisis." However, the increased price encouraged more conservation and a greater search for more petroleum. By the end of the 1990s, petroleum was priced at historical lows in constant dollars. However, in the 2000s, the price of crude oil again greatly increased with the economic development of China and India and the popularity of sport utility vehicles (SUVs) in the United States reversing conservation. As a result, the recovery and upgrading of extra heavy oil has been greatly stepped up in Venezuela and in Alberta, Canada, and new discoveries of oil have been made in West Africa and offshore Brazil. Instead of a shortage, the greatest threat to continuation of the Petroleum Age well into the twenty-first century is environmental.

There are concerns about the emission of sulfur oxides, nitrogen oxides, and carbon monoxide when the fuel is burned, about the dangers of accidental spills when it is transported and stored, and about air and water emissions when it is produced and refined. Even more importantly, both science and society are becoming aware that the burning of petroleum and other fossil fuels is producing enough carbon dioxide to cause global warming through a "greenhouse" effect.

As a result, most of us wish neither to cause a significant climate change nor to pay the energy cost of a complete shift away from fossil fuels.

With all this history of the technological exploitation of petroleum, there is a misconception that we completely understand petroleum and have reached the technological limits of its conversion to fuels and petrochemicals. Nothing can be further from the truth. This is especially the case for the larger molecules in petroleum, the macromolecules or heavy oil.1 The objective of the author in writing this book is to convey the richness of petroleum as a field of science and innovation. Although petroleum contains over a million different molecules, most of this diversity is in the heavy fraction, the macromolecules. Although physicists have recently initiated a new branch called the physics of complex materials, by comparison petroleum is an "ultracomplex" material. Even, some of the petroleum (asphaltenes) self organizes so that it is difficult to measure molecular weight. Petroleum is neither a solution nor a colloid, but a hybrid of both. The greatest attractive interaction is between polynuclear aromatic structures that are rarely found in other materials. During thermal processing, these polynuclear aromatic structures can form a discotic liquid crystalline phase, only an example of its challenging but interesting phase behavior. Although the high viscosity of oil provides its great lubricating properties, we have little understanding why the viscosity is so high. However, with all this uncertainty, the most surprising feature of petroleum is that it can be described by simple models. Although theory tells us that reactions of complex mixtures of molecules cannot be first order, the thermal reaction of petroleum macromolecules is first order with constant activation energy over the entire temperature range that we have been able to measure. Solubility parameters are known to be at best a rough predictor of the phase behavior of pure, small molecules, but they may describe the phase behavior of petroleum better than any other system. When we ignore all that molecular complexity and represent petroleum macromolecules as either a few pseudo components or being composed of only two building blocks, much of the thermal chemistry can be described quantitatively as well as we can measure it. These are not merely the result of empirical correlation because they describe changes in properties, reactor type, and initial concentrations. The excitement is in exploiting this surprising simplicity with new innovations as well as to unravel the underlying reasons using modern tools for studying macromolecules. Such an endeavor may even enable us to better understand ultracomplex materials other than just petroleum. [1]

6.3. Stages of Global Oil Development

As demonstrated in Bina (1985), the entire history of international oil during the twentieth century has gone through the three distinct stages of development. These are: the era of the early oil concessions, the era of "50–50 profit-sharing," and the era of unified global commoditization, and internationalization of the oil industry. On the domestic side (i.e., the US oil industry), one can recognize three different stages as well. The first stage in the development of oil in the United States saw a gradual emergence of horizontal and vertical integration in the industry that led to the formation of trusts and subsequent trust-busting tendencies, culminating in the antitrust law of 1911 (Keysen and Turner 1959). As we may observe from the history of oil production during almost three quarters of the twentieth century, both in the United States and elsewhere in the world, the cartel-like practices and the process of cartelization emerged as a formidable de facto institution (Stocking and Watkins 1948,

---

[1]Irwin A. Wiehe: Process Chemistry of Petroleum Macromolecules. Taylor & Francis Group, LLC. 2008. P 1:2

Stocking 1950, De Chazeau and Kahn 1959, Blair 1976, Engler 1977). The second stage in the development of the US oil industry is the neo-cartelization era of production control, which culminated in the establishment of the Interstate Compact Commission. This period, which emerged subsequent to the trust-busting landmark of 1911, ended in the early 1970s, with the emergence of the 1973–74 oil crisis that transformed the entire industry irrevocably. Finally, there is the era of trans nationalization of the oil industry (since 1974), which has rendered the US oil industry an inseparable part of the organic whole of global production and exchange in global competition. [1]

6.4. Colonial Concessions and the Cartelized Oil

In addition to the peculiar terms of the contract conducted between the rulers of the precapitalist oil rich nations and social entities in the Middle East and elsewhere—which, of course, put the question of national sovereignty on the front burner for a while, and later was counterbalanced with attempted oil nationalizations—in this early era, we can observe four additional historically specific

---

[1] Cyrus Bina: A Prelude to the Foundation of Political Economy. PALGRAVE MACMILLAN. 2013. P 87

characteristics (1) the existence of the concept of constant royalty in terms of a fixed sum per quantity of output, (2) the formation of joint ventures among oil companies for the purpose of joint control of new concessions, (3) the founding of the Achnacarry Agreement, and (4) the agreement of "posting" the price of oil, from anywhere in the world, based upon the wellhead price of oil at the US Gulf (of Mexico).

First, in contrast with the notion of economic rent that fundamentally emerges from the appropriation of surplus profits by virtue of the ownership of land or mineral deposits in the subsurface, the oil royalties of the early period were established on an arbitrary basis, often at four shillings per ton of crude oil, quite unrelated to its value or price (Cattan 1967a, 1967b). This is a significant phenomenon that should be considered as a first step, before the transformation of the oil industry in the Middle East, North Africa, Asia, and Latin America from a precapitalist to a growing capitalist industry, especially in the view of subsequent oil nationalizations in Mexico (1938), Iran (1951), and Iraq (1972).

Second, the early joint ventures among the transnational oil companies were not motivated primarily by concern over risk and capital requirements. Instead, these arrangements were the main instruments of joint control over substantial parts of the globe; they were intended for the direct control of the pace of utilization of oil reserves by a handful of private enterprises. The 1927 Redline Agreement by the IPC partners pertaining to the Iraqi oil concessions is a case in point (Blair 1976). It is noteworthy that the division of the world's oil resources has not been done solely according to individual company ownership, which implies the existence of a simple form of rivalry.

The pattern of joint ownership has also been dominant, such as the collective agreements pertaining to the Saudis' Aramco or the Iranian Consortium (Cattan 1967a, 1967b). Thus, one cannot rule out either rivalry or cooperation in the process of cartelization during this period.

Third, another feature of this early period is the necessity of discretionary agreements. Even though it is difficult to report all instances of the worldwide cartel-like arrangements among the major oil companies, the fully documented "As Is Agreement" of 1928, better known as Achnacarry Act, reveals a great deal about the collective effort of the companies in this period (Federal Trade

Commission, International Petroleum Cartel 1952).

Finally, for the purpose of pricing of direct intercompany oil transfers, the companies designated a set of administered prices called "posted prices." These administered prices were initially based on the production cost of crude oil in the Gulf of Mexico, formerly the center of gravity of international oil. Even though the share of Middle East oil production has increased significantly, as the center of gravity of the world's oil reserves had shifted to the Persian Gulf, the IPC had routinely charged the freight costs from the Gulf of Mexico even for the shipments that originated from the Persian Gulf.

However, as early as 1941, this practice was questioned by the British Admiralty. Similar objections were also raised, shortly after the Second World War, by the US administrators of Marshall Plan in Europe. Thus, the companies were forced to get rid of this phantom freight through recognition of the Persian Gulf as a second basingpoint in addition to the US Gulf. But, as the cheap Middle Eastern crude was able to penetrate further into the Western markets, the companies soon recognized that, because of the significant difference in the production costs of these two basing points, the establishment of a single global posted price might not be possible. This led to the birth of a double basing-point system, with two different cost structures, which included both Gulfs. Accordingly, there were different posted prices for these oil regions. Nevertheless, the Persian Gulf posted price was more reflective of the US oil cost-structure than of its own cost of production. In other words, the cost of oil from the Persian Gulf, including the cost of "royalties," has been a fraction of the cost of its counterpart at the Gulf of Mexico. This comparison is also relevant to the production costs at the Venezuelan oil fields, which has been substantially below the US costs, but nevertheless kept according to the cartel's yardstick at the Gulf of Mexico. [1]

6.5. Decartelization of Oil and Competition

Contrary to the US neo-cartelization era since 1911, the post cartelization era has been about the global commoditization of oil through competition. The price of oil, which once was the result of either the IPC's basing-point control abroad and the subject of the coordinated "market demand factor" strategy in

---

[1] Cyrus Bina: A Prelude to the Foundation of Political Economy. PALGRAVE MACMILLAN. 2013. P 88:89

the US domestic oil industry, now found a new footing in the budding spot markets around the world, as long-term colonial oil concessions were gradually yielding to the all-embracing and blind forces of the market. As the control of oil was about to be freed from the quivering clutches of the IPC, the dawn of a *new global oil order* was visible on the horizon; the reintegration of oil by means of global competition brought all oil producing regions of the world under one pricing rule. Thus, over and above the general rate of profit, the more productive oil regions could appropriate differential profits commensurate with their differential oil rents. This has since been a universal rule for OPEC producers and non-OPEC producers alike. In this new milieu, at the various oil regions, the "posted prices" that were lingering from the IPC era were forced to be in sync with each other. More important, these "prices" also were compelled to mirror the actual market conditions heralded by the now spreading spot oil markets around the globe.

Finally, the commencement of the decartelization era coincided with the 1973–74 oil crisis. But as it turned out, far from being an exception, the periodic crisis is a regular feature of any globally integrated system of capitalist production and reproduction. The oil crises in this new order are like a bellwether acting to announce the periodic restructuring of capital from time to time.

They are the Guardian Angels of capital, so to speak. As was pointed out earlier, since the decartelization of oil, there has been a fundamental transformation in the nature of OPEC. OPEC has developed into the structure of global oil. The limits of OPEC oil rent are also set by this structure, far from the combined intentions of its individual members or the collective actions of producers in this body.

And as has been implicitly or explicitly shown in this book, the size of oil rent is not determined by the action of OPEC but by the specific social and material forces that made oil a marvel of capitalism. [1]

6.6. SIZE AND RISK CONSIDERATIONS

Assuming that the funds are available and at reasonable cost; size, risk, and project viability considerations will ultimately dictate the lenders' commitment of funds. Some projects are in the order of $10 to $20 billion. Private lenders, because of the risk associated with such

---

[1] Cyrus Bina: A Prelude to the Foundation of Political Economy. PALGRAVE MACMILLAN. 2013. P 91:92

large-scale projects and the commitment of funds relative to the capital base may view these projects as just being too large. For example, by 1985, the total capital base of the banking system may approach $15-20 billion. If the banking system were to commit 20 percent of its base to energy projects, an upper limit of some $3-4 billion would be placed on their participation. Also, many large-scale projects may come along at the same time, causing "bunching problems." Lenders are concerned with the following types of risks: [1]

• *Technological Risks.* Resource projects are expensive because of the growing inaccessibility of natural resources: geographic inaccessibility, such as gas in the Arctic, or oil in the North Sea, or technical inaccessibility such as the tar sands and heavy oils. Many of the new projects today are based on technologies that have not as yet been commercially tested.

• *Project completion.* What happens if a project is not completed? Who picks up the responsibility for the debt? Although some risks can be offset, for example, by providing for

---

[1] W. T. Ziemba S. L. Schwartz: ENERGY POLICY MODELING: UNITED STATES AND CANADIAN EXPERIENCES Volume II. Martinus Nijhoff Publishing, Boston 1st edition 1980. P 352: 353

generous cost overruns, it is not possible to eliminate the risk entirely.

• *Operating risks.* Protection against a revenue shortfall from changed market conditions can be provided by take-or-pay contracts, all events cost-of-service contracts or working capital agreements. But, these too have their limitations.

• *Political risks.* Foreign lenders are becoming increasingly sensitive to the risk associated with the current debate on Confederation. If the situation were to continue indefinitely, the availability of large amounts of foreign capital for Canadian projects will likely be severely curtailed.

6.7. When Will Petroleum Run Out?

In 1977, when the author joined Exxon Corporate Research and three years after the Arab oil embargo, many people, including the petroleum companies, believed that we were running out of a reliable, secure supply of petroleum. At that time, OPEC refused to lower the price of petroleum. Shortages caused long lines at gas stations. Exxon and other petroleum companies were doing large-scale research and development on the conversion of coal and shale oil to hydrocarbon liquids.

In the 1980s the threat went away. In 1981 the average annual price of oil peaked at over $30 per barrel, and by 1986 the average annual price was close to $12 per barrel with short-term prices below $10 per barrel. There were no more gas lines, and Exxon ceased construction of a shale oil conversion plant in Colorado.

What happened? The sharp increase in the price of gasoline caused a large increase in conservation in the United States. Four-cylinder cars became popular, the U.S. government mandated an increase in automobile gas mileage over time from the automobile manufactures, and speed limits were reduced on highways.

The higher price of petroleum spurred the exploration and discovery of more petroleum all over the world, including in deeper seas. In June 1977, the first oil was pumped down the Trans-Alaska Pipeline that opened the Prudhoe Bay Field, the largest field of petroleum within the United States, over 13 billion barrels.

The demand for petroleum decreased by 5 million barrels per day by 1986, and the supply of petroleum by non-OPEC countries increased by 14 million barrels per day, causing the price to drop. In an attempt to recover OPEC control, Saudi Arabia flooded the market with petroleum. The world was far from running out of petroleum, but the laws of economics eventually worked their magic. Unfortunately, people proceeded to stick their heads in the sand and forgot there ever was a problem.

Now, in 2007, six-cylinder engines and SUVs are popular, the mandate on automobile gas mileage has been repealed, speed limits are back up, the production of petroleum from the Prudhoe Bay Field has peaked, and the price of petroleum has reached above $90 per barrel. Although the response of the U.S.

government has been slow, economic forces are responding. Active oil exploration has discovered oil fields in offshore West Africa, offshore Brazil, and in still deeper water of the Gulf of Mexico. The production of extra heavy oil has ramped up in Canada and Venezuela, biodiesel and gasoline-containing ethanol is being marketed, and hybrid cars have become popular. However, the production of petroleum peaked in United States in 1971, and the discovery of new conventional petroleum reserves in the world has not been keeping up with consumption. Is the supply of petroleum about to run out?

Paul Roberts, using well-balanced reporting, provides his reader with enough information to make guesses as to the future supply of petroleum. He arrives at the possibility that the production of non-OPEC petroleum could peak in 2015, and OPEC petroleum could peak in 2025. Of course, no one really knows. Even this guess is for conventional, light crude oil. As the price of petroleum increases, the search will move into still deeper oceans and into the Artic. More oil will be extracted from existing wells where past recoveries have been only 25 to 33%. Of course, the huge resources of extra heavy oil in Alberta, Canada, and in Venezuela are only beginning to be tapped. Liquid hydrocarbons are already being manufactured from natural gas in a few locations. Although fuels from agricultural products will never replace the huge consumption volumes of petroleum, they can make a significant contribution. Ethanol from cellulose, such as switchgrass, is much more promising than from corn. Butanol may be preferred over ethanol because of its lower solubility in water and higher solubility in gasoline. Biodiesel from canola oil produced from rapeseed (the third most produced vegetable oil in the world) is more promising than that from soybean oil because of the former's higher production per acre. Of course, the technologies for obtaining liquid hydrocarbons from the conversion of shale oil and coal are on the shelf, waiting to be reactivated. Therefore, although we are not likely to run out of liquid hydrocarbon fuels for a very long time, cheap, light petroleum is a very limited natural resource. Petroleum price is already high enough to activate alternatives, but the prospects are that the price will increase further in the future to maintain a high supply of liquid hydrocarbon fuels, which include even more expensive alternatives. Clearly, the time for greater conservation is already here.

What about hydrogen? Unfortunately, there are no hydrogen reservoirs that can be tapped by drilling a well. It is most economically produced from natural gas or from hydrocarbon liquids of petroleum. Hydrogen from water is far from energy efficient unless it involves reactions with carbonaceous materials (gasification).

It is the preferred fuel for fuel cells if their technical obstacles can be overcome to achieve their high theoretical efficiencies. Even in this case, for vehicles the hydrogen will likely be made onboard by reforming liquid hydrocarbons to carry safely enough fuel in a limited volume. Although this method promises to conserve hydrocarbons by the much higher fuel efficiency, fuel cells operating on hydrogen do not completely free us from our dependence on petroleum. [1]

7. Oil and gas production in some countries

7.1. Oil and gas production in Nigeria

Nigeria has considerable reserves of conventional energy resources. It is one of the world's largest producers of oil and it has the largest reserves of natural gas in the African Continent. It therefore became the world's fourth leading exporter of liquefied natural gas (LNG) in 2012. Nigeria is also a member of the Organization of the Petroleum Exporting Countries (OPEC), which it joined in 1971 after over 10 years of oil production that began in the late 1950s. Coal reserves stand at 2.175 billion tons, but production has long since ceased (in the 1950s) as the government has concentrated on the oil and gas resources.

Nigeria is also rich in tar sand or oil sand, which is a combination of clay, sand, water, and bitumen (a heavy black viscous oil). Tar sands can be mined and processed to extract

---

[1]Irwin A. Wiehe: Process Chemistry of Petroleum Macromolecules. Taylor & Francis Group, LLC. 2008. P 6:8

the oil-rich bitumen, which can be refined into oil (Oil Shale and Tar Sands Programmatic. [1]

Despite the large energy resources in Nigeria, energy consumption is relatively low compared with other African countries with comparable energy resources. This low energy consumption is due to the recurrent scarcity of petroleum products at vehicle petrol stations, while frequent electricity "black-outs" have resulted in a high reliance by the Nigerian populace on personal electricity generators.

Despite the scarcity of petroleum products, energy demand has been increasing in Nigeria, because of the increase in economic development and the population growth. According to Sambo et al. (2006), the major driver behind increasing energy demand is the population growth, while the most important determinant is the level of economic activity, measured by the country's gross domestic product (GDP).

Nigeria's population is projected to grow from 178,516,904 (as of 2014) to 440,355,062 by 2050. To address the needs of

---

[1] Nnaemeka Vincent Emodi: Energy Policies for Sustainable Development Strategies. Springer Science+Business Media Singapore 2016. P 12

this increasing population, the Energy Commission of Nigeria (ECN) analyzed the country's energy sector from 2000 to 2030 using the Wien Automatic System Planning (WASP) package and the Model for Analysis of Energy Demand (MAED). [1]

In Nigeria, commercial production of crude oil began in 1958 based on proven recoverable reserves of 1.48×106 billion tons. Production rose from an initial quantity of 3.1 million metric tons to 20.3 million tons in 1960, 54.2 million tons by 1970, and 104.1 million tons in 1980, all in response to demand from international markets rather than from domestic demand. On average, local consumption accounted for just 3 % of production, while the remaining 97 % was exported. Since 1980, three domestic petroleum refineries have supplied petroleum products for local consumption: the Kaduna Refinery with a capacity of 110,000 bbl/d (barrels per day), Port Harcourt Refinery with a capacity of 210,000 bbl/d, and Warri Refinery with a capacity of 125,000 bbl/d. the production of crude oil in Nigeria increased rapidly between 1980 and 2012; however, the rate of increase was dependent on the economic and geopolitical situations in both producing and

---

[1]Nnaemeka Vincent Emodi: Energy Policies for Sustainable Development Strategies. Springer Science+Business Media Singapore 2016. P 13

consuming countries. Nigeria's current production capacity of 2.4 million bbl/d remains low because of problems in the Niger Delta and OPEC production restrictions. However, projections have placed future (2030) production at over 5.0 million bbl/d. [1]

Crude oil production in Nigeria

Crude oil production reached its peak in 2005 but has subsequently declined significantly because of the activities of militants

[1] Nnaemeka Vincent Emodi: Energy Policies for Sustainable Development Strategies. Springer Science+Business Media Singapore 2016. P 17

in the Niger Delta region. These activities came to a halt in 2009 when amnesty was granted to the militants and by 2010, oil production began to increase as oil companies began operating at full capacity. The Nigerian government also took drastic measures to attract investment in deep-water acreage in order to diversify the location of oil fields and increase oil production. This has resulted in the production of an additional 800,000 bbl/d since 2003. However, crude oil production declined from 2011 to 2012 because of heavy floods and supply disruptions.

In addition to the challenges faced by the government, the indigenes of the Niger Delta region suffer from the effects of environmental damages resulting from pipeline vandalism. When pipelines are vandalized, crude oil is stolen to supply illegal refineries. The result is environmental degradation and the risk of a pipeline explosion for local communities. The rates of domestic production and export of crude oil did not improve significantly between 2006 and 2014 because of the issue of crude oil theft.

The oil price in Nigeria has been in line with the OPEC price and has fared well over the years, reaching its peak in 2008, but declining in 2009. The price of oil in Nigeria was US$102.33 per barrel in August 2014; however, with the recent fall in the crude oil price, which is US$53 for West Texas Intermediate (WTI) and US$57.33 for Brent crude, the country's economy will be adversely affected. The previous rise in the crude oil price was due to high oil consumption in countries such as China and India, in conjunction with conflict in key oil exporting countries such as Libya. [1]

High oil prices induced companies in Canada and the United States (US) to start drilling for new hard to extract crude in North Dakota's shale formations and Alberta's oil sands. This has resulted in a "Price-War" between OPEC and the US. The US, which was the largest single importer of crude oil from Nigeria in 2012, ceased importing oil at the end of 2014. Other countries have also reduced their oil imports from Nigeria, including the countries of the European Union.

Fuel subsidies cost the Nigerian government US$8 billion in 2011 alone, which constituted 30 % of federal government expenditure, 4 % of the country's GDP, and 118 % of the capital budget. However, the Nigerian government removed the fuel subsidy on the 1st of January 2012. Subsequently, oil consumption

---

[1] Nnaemeka Vincent Emodi: Energy Policies for Sustainable Development Strategies. Springer Science+Business Media Singapore 2016. P 18: 20

in Nigeria has increased. Downstream industries in Nigeria, which include domestic refineries and various petrochemical industries, use the crude oil produced in Nigeria. These refineries produce products such as linear alkyl benzene, benzene, heavy alkylate, and deparaffinated kerosene for domestic consumption.

The estimated proven reserves of natural gas in Nigeria stand at 182 trillion cubic feet (TCF) with a mean gauge pressure of about 12 bars, a calorific value of 35 mJ/m^3, and a mean specific volume of 1.56×10^{-3} m^3/kg. In 2012, the production rate was about 1.35 TCF of dry natural gas, making Nigeria the 25th largest producer of dry natural gas in the world. [1]

Natural gas reserves are located in the Niger Delta region of Nigeria (South- South). In the past, Nigeria flared about 73 % of its gas because of poor infrastructure, which placed Nigeria second in the list of gas-flaring countries. However, because of the efforts of the Nigerian government to reduce gas flaring through the financing and provision of relevant infrastructure to use the previously flared gas, Nigeria is now 365th on the list. Infrastructure that uses the previously flared gas includes the

---

[1]Nnaemeka Vincent Emodi: Energy Policies for Sustainable Development Strategies. Springer Science+Business Media Singapore 2016. P 20

power sector, which accounts for 80 % of the total domestic consumption and generates 81 % of the total electricity supply in Nigeria. [1]

Europe has reduced its LNG imports from Nigeria since 2012, whereas the US has completely stopped importing from Nigeria because of increasing domestic production. However, imports have increased in Asian countries such as Japan, South Korea, and India, while France, Spain, Portugal, Taiwan, and Turkey still maintain their LNG imports from Nigeria. In 2013, there was supply disruption and a temporary blockade on Nigeria's LNG shipments, which led to a fall in its production and export; however, this did not affect domestic consumption. [2]

7.2. Oil and gas production in Egypt

Energy will continue to play an important role in Egypt's economy in the coming decade. While oil exports have been declining as production has fallen at mature oil fields and domestic consumption has risen, natural gas

[1] Nnaemeka Vincent Emodi: Energy Policies for Sustainable Development Strategies. Springer Science+Business Media Singapore 2016. P 21
[2] Nnaemeka Vincent Emodi: Energy Policies for Sustainable Development Strategies. Springer Science+Business Media Singapore 2016. P 24

exports are expected to become a major source of hard currency revenues over the next decade.

Egypt produced an average of about 631,616 barrels per day (bbl/d) of crude oil in 2002, down sharply from 748,000 bbl/d in 2000, but only slightly below the 639,260 bbl/d produced in 2001. Egyptian crude oil production had peaked at 922,000 bbl/d in 1996. Demand for petroleum products has declined slightly since 1998, after rapid growth during the previous five-year period. This is due in part to the weakness of the economy, but also to reductions in subsides for petroleum products consumption and the increased use of compressed natural gas (CNG) as a fuel for motor vehicles. Egypt hopes that exploration activity, particularly in new areas, will discover sufficient oil in the coming years to slow the decline in output. Egyptian oil production comes from 4 main areas: The Gulf of Suez (about 60%), the Western Desert, the Eastern Desert, and the Sinai Peninsula.

In the early nineties, 189 discoveries were achieved, including 89 gas discoveries. Such discoveries made the Mediterranean a "sedimentary basin by international standard" resulting in huge development in Egypt's natural gas reserves, which amounted to over 37 TCF by the beginning of 1999; compared to over 17 TCF approx. in 1992 and 6.3 TCF approx. in 1982.

The rapid rise in natural gas reserves has led to a search for export options, which has become particularly important to Egypt's future international balance of payments due to the decline in oil exports. In late 1999, the Egyptian government stated that natural gas reserves were more than sufficient for domestic needs, and that foreign firms producing gas in Egypt should seek export customers.

By the rise of the new millennium, Egypt achieved a successful effort in the field of gas exploration as its proven gas reserves have reached around 62 TCF with probable reserves of 120 TCF. This encouraged the ministry of Petroleum to formulate a balanced strategy that satisfies the local market needs and opens new regional and international markets without trading off the future generation needs. Such sustainable development strategy shall achieve the national objectives that include: efficient utilization of the natural resources, economic development as well environmental protection. [1]

---

[1] Dr.Mansour Soliman: NATURAL GAS: INVESTMENT STRATEGIES IN AN UNCERTAIN WORLD. P 4: 6

The ministry of petroleum is giving first priority to availing the domestic market requirements. A strategic plan is being developed to identify new policies that can accelerate the efficient local use of gas (e.g., evaluation of existing barriers and a review of the major economic and energy sector trends). Specifically, the aim is to assist in the development of policy and market-based solutions that can stimulate gas use in the industrial and commercial sectors. The Egyptian Natural Gas Holding (EGAS) Company, which oversees the development and growth of the gas industry, will play a leading role in this respect.

Developing local markets for gas can create new investment opportunities that stimulate economic growth, increase industrial competitiveness, create new jobs, and free-up crude oil for export.

The gas demand estimates show an increase in the domestic consumption to over 3500 million cf/d by 2010, to increase gradually thereafter in order to cope with the requirement of electric power generation stations, as well as those of the industries and the industrial areas, presently on-stream or projected to be supplied with gas as a fuel and / or raw materials requirements for fertilizers, petrochemicals and iron & steel industries.

There are main policies and market initiatives that are being evaluated as part of the strategic plan. Each of these initial policy options will be analyzed in terms of their potential fit within the local market and their ability to generate economic and environmental gains. These preliminary policies and market initiatives include:

Pricing schemes: the subsidization of local energy prices is a major expenditure for the GOE- this includes the subsidy of fuel prices in the industrial and commercial sector. Potential new pricing schemes can be used to gradually and consistently move fuel prices over time towards the full recovery of economic costs.

Cogeneration policy: the feasibility of cogeneration projects Is currently limited by a lack of a defined policy that allow for cogeneration units that operate in parallel to the electric grid and to buy-and- sell back power at an economic price. Previous market studies have estimated that operating in parallel can increase cogeneration capital costs by an average of 25% (due to the over-sizing of units). In addition, the inability of a cogeneration developer to sell their excess electricity back to the utility limits the financial viability of cogeneration investments and hinders their ability to achieve an appropriate thermal-to-electric ratio. The establishment of a cogeneration policy should be linked to the country's economic development plans in particular encouraging the use of cogeneration in new industrial cities or tourism zones that are geographically isolated areas.

Market initiatives: market-based solutions can be used to help increase the local supply of and demand for natural gas energy services and high efficiency technologies. One objective in the design of market initiatives is to develop solutions that can be revenue neutral to the GOE. Results from a market study conducted in a new industrial city indicate that LDCs can benefits from high-return investments that meet a growing demand for integrated energy services. To achieve revenue 8 neutrality, one potential option is to link the development of given investment incentive to new pricing schemes (e.g. funding an incentive from the potential gradual removal of fuel price subsidies). [1]

In geological terms, there are three main productive basins, of which by far the largest is the offshore Gulf of Suez, where oil is trapped beneath Miocene salt. Although now a very mature basin, modern technology has

---

[1] Dr.Mansour Soliman: NATURAL GAS: INVESTMENT STRATEGIES IN AN UNCERTAIN WORLD. P 8: 10

improved the mapping of the sub-salt plays, which may possibly lead to a few more modest finds. Another basin lies in the El Alemein area of western Egypt where Jurassic source-rocks have charged Cretaceous reservoirs in easterly trending rift zones. The third basin is the Nile Delta, which is a gas province. The Mediterranean shelf is narrow and steep. It might hold some Deepwater potential, but the chances are slim. [1]

Oil production commenced in 1914 but did not rise significantly until after the Second World War with the discoveries in the Gulf of Suez. It passed 500 kb/d in 1979 to reach a peak of 922 kb/d in 1996, since when it has declined to 523 kb/d in 2010. It will likely continue to decline in the future at about 4.35% a year. Consumption has risen steeply in recently years to reach 270 Mb/a, meaning that the country has become a net importer.

Gas production commenced in 1935 and reached an early plateau at around 1 Gcf a year from 1941 to 1953 before falling steeply. A second surge of production came with the opening of the offshore in the Nile Delta to climb steeply over the last few years to reach 2

---

[1]C.J. Campbell: Campbell's Atlas of Oil and Gas Depletion. Colin J. Campbell and Alexander Wöstmann 2013. P 39

Tcf a year in 2010. Consumption has risen in parallel, with supply being dedicated to the domestic market. Along with related gas liquids, it will be an increasingly important source of energy for the population centers of Cairo and Alexandria. Both, oil and gas production is expected to fall over the next year or two as a consequence of the fall of the last government and political uncertainty. [1]

Hosni Mobarak pursued a moderate policy, concentrating on economic development, on which progress has been countered by the effects of an exploding population. There remained an undercurrent of deep frustration by those seeking to restore Arab confidence. It exploded in January 2011 in the face of an economic recession caused by growing oil imports and higher oil prices, and led to the removal of President Mobarak. The country remains in a relatively unstable condition without a new strong government.

The country has become a net importer of oil as domestic production continues to fall. But gas production can be maintained, and the country is blessed with a high level of solar radiation, which could help provide for its

---

[1] C.J. Campbell: Campbell's Atlas of Oil and Gas Depletion. Colin J. Campbell and Alexander Wöstmann 2013. P 40

energy needs over the next few decades. Looking ahead it would be reasonable to expect growing Egyptian pressure on Libya, its oil-rich neighbor, which may take the form of close cooperation or, if that fails, outright hostility. [1]

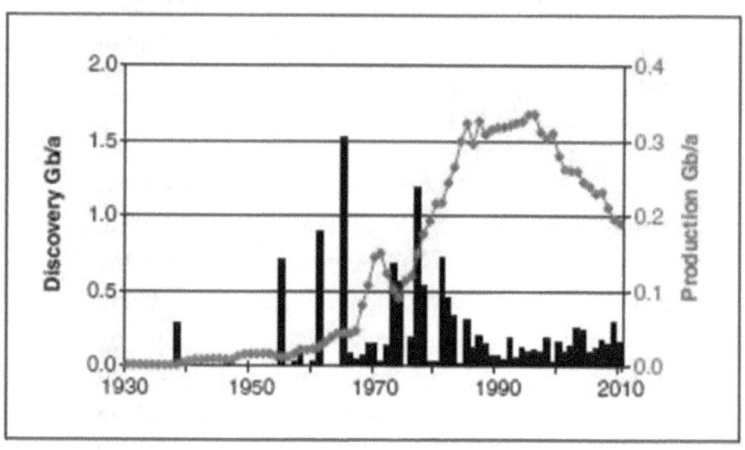

Egypt discovery and production

The gas oil production in local market was developed from 4139 thousand ton (th.T) at 1991 to 8276 th. T at 2003, the difference represents an increase in the production yield reached to 100 % of the production at 1991. The development was due to improve the performance of the existing atmospheric

---

[1] C.J. Campbell: Campbell's Atlas of Oil and Gas Depletion. Colin J. Campbell and Alexander Wöstmann 2013. P 41

distillation units and also due to install a new refiner (MIDOR) stared in operation at 2001 which contain a hydrocracker unit and produce about 25 % of the total gas oil production in Egypt.

Another addition to local gas oil production was a mild Hydrocracker that installed at (AMOC) company which designed to produce 460 th.T/y of high quality gas oil. In spite of increasing the production of gas oil and the addition of a new operating units aiming to maximize gas oil production rate, the consumption was increased by rates come over the production rates. [1]

---

[1]Marawan , H.: Maximization of Egyptian Gas Oil Production Through the Optimal Use of the Operating Parameters. P 2: 4

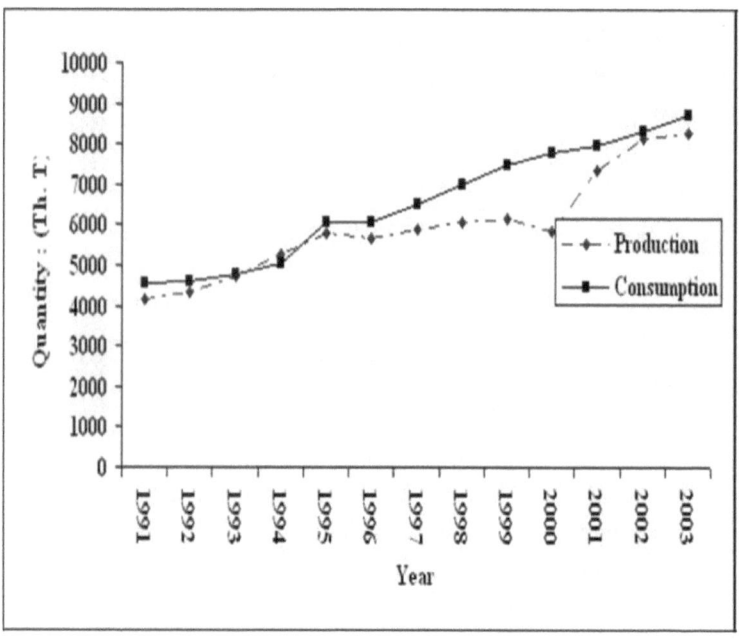

7.3. Oil and gas production in Australia

Australia formed part of the Permian super-continent, known as Pangea, before it began drifting southeastwards during the Triassic, about 180 million years ago. It reached its present position some 50 million years ago, when Antarctica split off to continue its geotectonic voyage to the South Pole. The early separation has given Australia a unique flora and fauna. It is noteworthy that fossils of some of the first forms of life on the planet have been found in Australia.

Much of the continent is made up of ancient shield rocks, but they are flanked by two Tertiary petroleum systems: The Bass Strait Basin off the south coast and the extensive NW Shelf. There are, in addition, interior Palaeozoic basins of minor potential. The NW Shelf forms the passive margin of the continent facing the contact with the Eurasian Plate, bordering the Indonesian island arc. It is made up of a thick sequence of Mesozoic and Tertiary sediments. Several rather lean source-rock intervals have been identified in the Mesozoic sequence, but in many areas lie below the oil generating window, explaining the preponderance of gas condensate finds. [1]

There was some earlier production that escaped the records, but significant production commenced in the 1960s and reached a peak of 722 kb/d in 2000, some 33 years after peak discovery. It has since declined to 436 kb/d, being set to continue to decline at about 3% a year. About 180 Tcf of gas has been discovered, of which 32 Tcf have been produced. Production stands at about 1.7 Tcf/a.

Assuming that production rises at 10% a year, it could reach a plateau of about 5 Tcf/a

---

[1]C.J. Campbell: Campbell's Atlas of Oil and Gas Depletion. Colin J. Campbell and Alexander Wöstmann 2013. P 75: 76

lasting from 2020 to 2040 before a final fall. Such a depletion pro fi le would give a total of 220 Tcf, assuming future discovery of almost 37.5 Tcf.

The gas also yields a substantial amount of gas-liquids, contributing about half the total liquid production by 2010. It is evident that Australia will increasingly rely on its substantial gas resources which are at an early stage of depletion.

Oil consumption stands at 351 Mb/a, meaning that Australia already has to import about one quarter of its needs, a percentage set to increase in the future as production declines. All of its gas production is consumed internally, apart from that used for LNG production. [1]

---

[1] C.J. Campbell: Campbell's Atlas of Oil and Gas Depletion. Colin J. Campbell and Alexander Wöstmann 2013. P 76

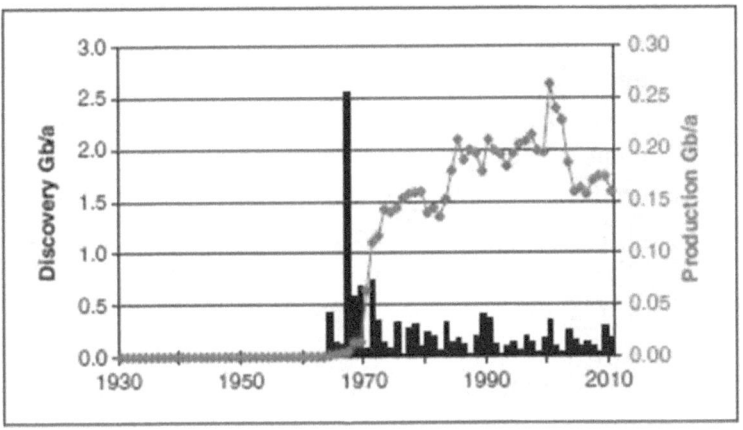

Australia discovery and production

7.4. Oil and gas production in china

China lies between the Siberian Shield and the Pacific Oceanic Plate. It is broadly divided into two provinces. In the remote west behind the Himalayas, lie several compressional basins, including the large Tarim Basin, which has a deep prospective Palaeozoic sequence, whereas to the east lie a series of Mesozoic and Tertiary basins, bounded by a major shear zone. They in turn give way to a large continental shelf bordering several back-arc basins at the edge of the Paci fi c Plate. [1]

---

[1]C.J. Campbell: Campbell's Atlas of Oil and Gas Depletion. Colin J. Campbell and Alexander Wöstmann

Oil production commenced in 1939 and rose gradually to 1964. It increased markedly thereafter, passing 1 Mb/d in 1973 to reach an overall peak at 4 Mb/d in 2010. At that point, some 56% of the estimated resource had been produced, suggesting that it is set to decline in the years ahead at the current Depletion Rate of about 5% a year. In earlier years, production operations were not blessed with the most advanced technology, but those limitations were partly compensated for by close drilling.

Gas production has followed a similar path to reach current production of about 3.3 Tcf/a. China's oil use has been growing rapidly to stand at about 3,354 Mb/a today. It means that the country has to import about half of its needs, being second only to the United States in total consumption. Close to 15 million new cars have taken to the roads over the past 12 months, and the demand for fuel obviously grows in parallel. Imports have thus risen to 1,866 Mb/a and are set to grow still higher as indigenous production declines, which explains why Chinese companies are scouring the world for exploration rights. The country's growing dependence on imported energy threatens its economic prosperity, which may slump in the future.

2013. P 129

Gas consumption stands at about 3.8 Tcf/a, which is set to expand as new pipelines are constructed. [1]

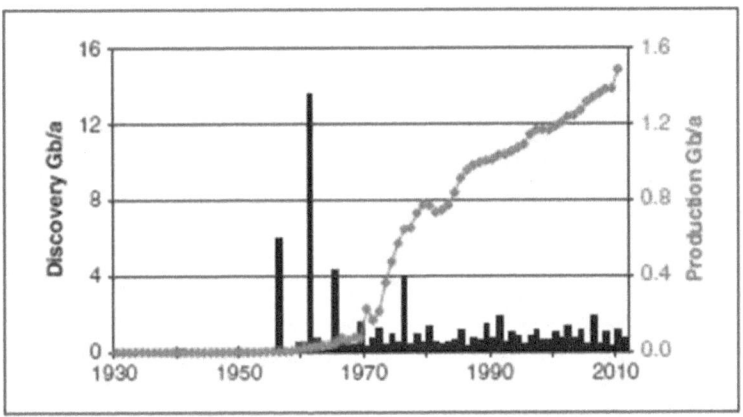

China discovery and production

As early as 1974, Dean (1974) considered the energy situation in the People's Republic of China and argued that the discovery and initial exploration of new petroleum reserves were significant changes to energy policy and operation. In particular, he was concerned with future developments in the energy industry and the effect on the international energy market. He argued that the size of China's fossil fuel and

---

([1])C.J. Campbell: Campbell's Atlas of Oil and Gas Depletion. Colin J. Campbell and Alexander Wöstmann 2013. P 130

hydroelectric resources, combining with the commitment to 'selfreliance' made it unlikely that China would become a major energy importer.

Furthermore, he argued that China would likely become a major exporter in the foreseeable future. By 1992 China had, in fact, become a major energy importer. Dorian and Clark (1987) discussed potential supply problems and implications for China's energy resources. They stated that primary energy production must increase significantly by the year 2000 if China was to achieve its current modernization and economic objectives. To support and sustain this rapid economic growth, indigenous supplies of primary energy resources would have to be developed at rates greater than those of the time. With a specific concern for China's sustainable. energy supplies, they conducted a systematic assessment of China's primary energy resources by Province using the Unit Regional Production Value (URPV) technique, originally developed by Griffiths (1978). What is interesting is that they present the potential for petroleum, natural gas, coal and uranium by Province and detailed URPV of petroleum, natural gas and coal see, Dorian and Clark (1987). Once they had identified the potential supply of petroleum, natural gas and coal by Province they considered the extent to which exploration is restricted by outdated equipment and poor management. Furthermore, they consider whether increased energy production may be limited by inadequate infrastructure combined with high capital requirements, safety and environmental issues. [1]

Compared with resource endowments, natural gas constitutes a small part in China's primary energy production structure. Yet, in recent years, the production appears to blowout. In 2012, China's natural gas production reached 107 billion cubic meters, increasing by 2.9 times than that of 2000 with an annual growth rate of 12 %. In primary energy consumption structure, the proportion of natural gas is still on the rise. However, domestic natural gas is not able to meet the requirement and import volume began to increase year by year. In 2012, China net natural gas import volume is 44.2 billion cubic meters. [2]

---

[1] Hengyun Ma l Les Oxley: China's Energy Economy. Springer-Verlag Berlin Heidelberg 2012. P 49: 50
[2] Jinjun Xue • Zhongxiu Zhao • Yande Dai • Bo Wang: Green Low-Carbon Development in China. Springer International Publishing Switzerland 2013. P 85

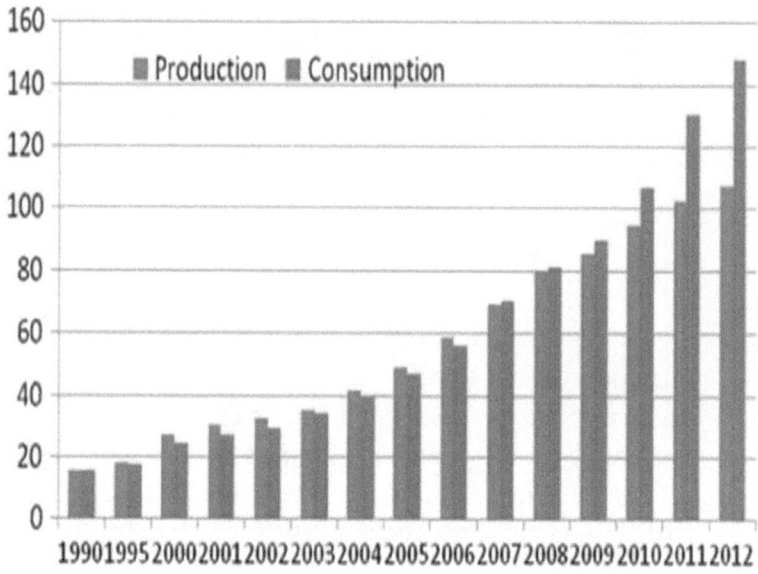

From the current situation of domestic energy resources, China is rich in coal resource and quite lack of oil and natural gas. Up to the end of 2011, proved recoverable coal reserve is 114.5 billion-ton, accounting for 13.3 % of the world recoverable reserves, oil 2 billion ton, 0.9 %, natural gas 3,100 billion cubic meter, 1.5 %. Due to huge population base, energy resource per capita in China is far below the world average level. In the end of 2011, coal resource per capital of China is 85 t per person, merely 69 % of the world average level, oil 1.5 t per person, only 4.4 % of world average level, natural gas 2,301 cubic meter per person, barely 7.7 % of the world average level. According to the output at present, China's coal reserve-production ratio is less than 33 years, oil 10 years and natural gas 30 years. [1]

	Production capacity	World rankings	Recoverable reserves by the end of the year	World ranking	Reserve-production ratio
Coal(100 million ton)	35.2	1	1,145	3	33
Oil (million ton)	2.03	5	20	15	9.9
Natural (100 million cubic meter)	1,026.9	6	31,000	13	29.8

Resource: National Bureau of Statistics of China, BP Statistical Review of World Energy 2012

As the sharp increase of vehicle population, China's demand on oil in the future will continue to rise. However, it is regarded that, crude oil production in China has entered into a stable peak, that is, except for discovery of large major reservoirs, it will not increase in a large extent. Under the condition of limited domestic crude oil, crude oil dependence on foreign countries continues to rise and the situation is hard to change. Therefore, development strategy and guideline of China's oil industry in the future is: pay great efforts to save, strengthen exploration, conduct import and replace in large scale. [2]

([1])Jinjun Xue • Zhongxiu Zhao • Yande Dai • Bo Wang: Green Low-Carbon Development in China. Springer International Publishing Switzerland 2013. P 94: 95
([2])Jinjun Xue • Zhongxiu Zhao • Yande Dai • Bo Wang:

7.5. Oil and gas production in Russia

Much of the eastern part of the country is underlain by the Siberian Shield, composed of ancient non-prospective rocks. A Permian tectonic plate boundary gave rise to the Urals Mountain. [1]

Early oil production is unsure and also confused because it does not distinguish the different regions of the former Soviet Union, but it is estimated that about one billion barrels had been produced by 1937, at which date production had risen to about 350 kb/d. It fell steeply during the latter years of the Second World War but rose thereafter passing a low of 1 Mb/d in 1956 to reach an overall peak of 11.36 Mb/d in 1983. It then collapsed with the fall of the Soviet Government to 5.9 Mb/d in 1998, before recovering to 8.7 Mb/d in 2010, at which point 65% of the assessed endowment had been produced, if we exclude, by definition, Polar production. In part, the recent rise was making good the production that would have already been secured but for the dislocations accompanying the fall of the Soviet regime.

Green Low-Carbon Development in China. Springer International Publishing Switzerland 2013. P 99
[1]C.J. Campbell: Campbell's Atlas of Oil and Gas Depletion. Colin J. Campbell and Alexander Wöstmann 2013. P 149

Production is now expected to commence its terminal decline at almost 4% a year. But for the anomalous fall in production, the overall peak would have been passed in the 1990s.

Oil consumption is currently running at 1,072 Mb/a, making the country a substantial exporter of 2,106 Mb/a. But on present trends and assessments, export capacity will fall to zero by around 2015 or even sooner if domestic consumption should increase faster than expected.150

In earlier years, associated gas must have been substantially flared, but after the Second World War it began to be exploited as a fuel for heating and electricity generation. Production in sub-Arctic Russia grew steadily to peak in 1991 at 22 Tcf a year, but has since fallen to about half that amount, as Arctic supplies rose to a dominant position.

It is difficult to forecast the future but it is here assumed that new sub-Arctic production will indeed be brought on stream to reach a plateau at about 25 Tcf/a by 2015, at the indicated midpoint of depletion. [1]

---

[1]C.J. Campbell: Campbell's Atlas of Oil and Gas Depletion. Colin J. Campbell and Alexander Wöstmann 2013. P 150

Geography has always played a vital role in the economics of Russia's oil sector. The necessity to transport oil more than 2000 miles from inland core production areas to domestic and export markets has posed difficult infrastructure challenges and significant transportation costs. The Soviet response to the challenge between the 1950s and 1980s was to create one of the world's largest integrated systems of large-diameter oil pipelines, presently run by Transneft, Russia's state oil transportation monopoly. The Transneft network has been the workhorse of the Russian economy, delivering crude oil from West Siberia, Volga-Urals, and Timan-Pechora, Russia's key oil production provinces, to markets at home and abroad. These flows have been primarily oriented towards Russia's refineries located in the European part of the country, refineries in Eastern Europe supplied by the Soviet legacy Druzhba pipeline, and Russia's marine export terminals in the Baltic Sea and the Black Sea, which deliver crude primarily to Western Europe and Mediterranean customers. During this period, oil production in East Siberia and Russia's Far East was relatively minor.

Things started to change in the mid-1990s, with 'the pivot to the east' occurring in three distinctive stages. The development of the Sakhalin oil and gas fields and the beginning of oil exports to Asia-Pacific (mid- 1990s to mid-

2000s) was followed by the construction of the ESPO oil pipeline (with Phase 1 capacity of 1 mmbd) and the development of the oil fields in East Siberia and Krasnoyarsk for the first phase of ESPO pipeline exports (2006–11). Since then, infrastructure development has focused on expanding ESPO capacity to 1.6 mmbd, creating a network of connecting upstream and downstream feeder pipelines, and developing the second generation of oil fields in the Krasnoyarsk-Yamal cluster to feed the expanded ESPO (2012–present). ESPO was a logical major step in the evolution of Russia's oil strategy. It connects the existing Transneft pipeline system with the newly developed regions in East Siberia and extends it towards export markets in China and the wider Asia-Pacific region, opening up an entirely new market for Russian crude oil. [1]

---

[1] Leo Lester: Energy Relations and Policy Making in Asia. 2016. P 60: 61

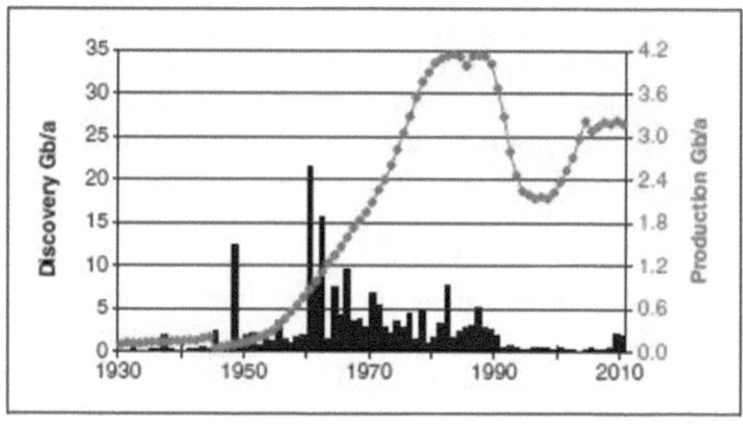

Russia discovery and production

Despite gloomy forecasts, both the region's administration and the companies involved in the oil and gas industry in Tomsk Oblast have several strategic options available to them to contend with the increasing decline of brownfield projects.

Before tackling the structure of the region's oil and gas industry and how it influences the administration's socio-economic plans, it may be helpful to look at the region's production in a federal context. The table below outlines Tomsk's oil and natural gas production in comparison with other regions, either currently or in the future that are earmarked to begin production of oil and natural gas.

The opportunity to explore the east bank of Tomsk Oblast's Ob River for hydrocarbon reserves may provide strategic options for both regional firms and the Oblast administration. According to the Oblast's Deputy Director for Administration, Tomsk's policy in coordination with federal authorities to open up the region for seismic surveys has been a success, even though results for the surveys are still pending. Capital inlay in projects involving resource management, geological surveying and the rehabilitation of existing wells has already totaled 21b RR. [1]

In terms of production, the regional leadership has made a conscious effort to diversify upstream production by allowing small companies to explore and invest in the next set of greenfield projects. Although this could be considered a major gamble – bearing in mind the way in which federal authorities and domestic energy majors have treated competitors in the past – this diversification strategy may pay off in terms of reducing regional economic dependence on Rosneft for tax revenue.

It may also provide impetus for further regionally based development of the upstream,

---

[1] Marja Jarvela • Sirkku Juhola: Energy, Policy, and the Environment. Springer Science+Business Media, LLC 2011. P 69: 70

away from old fields. Additionally, it may advance diversification of refining and service-oriented business activities in the value-added sectors and the downstream, thus guaranteeing an expanded tax base for future economic growth.

The second step is to determine just how the expected rise in benefits accrued from the region's resources will be spent. Here, there are some institutional pitfalls that need to be avoided. The Oblast administration has given consideration to improving the overall environment for businesses in order to spur investment away from the resource extraction sector to a diversified value-added, knowledge-based economy. However, increased budgetary revenues do not necessarily guarantee that bureaucrats or businesses will comply with the long-term vision of the regional executive and opt for short-term rent extraction strategies. [1]

We can indicate characteristics to sum up the main features of the previously developed approach: [2]

---

[1] Marja Jarvela • Sirkku Juhola: Energy, Policy, and the Environment. Springer Science+Business Media, LLC 2011. P 80: 81

[2] Rossella Bardazzi • Maria Grazia Pazienza Alberto Tonini: European Energy and Climate Security. Springer International Publishing Switzerland 2016. P 83

• a commitment to switching from one oil and gas province (as it becomes more mature) to another new one. The path of development from the 1930s to now has followed this pattern. First it was the Volga-Ural petroleum province, then Western Siberia and the Far East, together with the shelf area of the Arctic and far eastern seas. The main driving idea is to find and put into production new fresh reserves of better quality (bigger, lighter, easier to extract) as fast as possible; but among many other negative effects was the transportation distance from the fields to the main industrial centers (the same problem applies to exports);

• a main emphasis on locating and rapidly developing major and giant fields taking advantage of economies of scale. Economies of scale not only allow cheap extraction of oil from the subsoil but also compensate the high transport costs arising from growing distances. Moreover, they allow huge economic rents to be extracted;

• creation of the capacity to produce hydrocarbons aimed not only at domestic consumption but also for export to other countries. This feature is also a by-product of the economies of scale approach (the abundant oil and gas reserves discovered in the 1950s–1970s were much bigger than any possible consumption within the USSR, and afterwards in Russia);

• because of the planned economy, a single tightly-integrated infrastructure to deliver, process and transport oil, petroleum products and natural gas was built from the oil and gas provinces to existing refineries (and quite often to refineries which could process oil of a certain quality from a certain area).

7.6. Oil and gas production in Canada

Most of country overlies the non-prospective rocks of the Canadian Shield, but there are three petroleum systems. First is the Western Canadian Sedimentary Basin, lying mainly in Alberta, which relies largely on Palaeozoic source rocks, but is now at a mature stage of depletion so far as *Regular Conventional Oil* is concerned. Second is the Atlantic Margin off Newfoundland, which has Upper Jurassic source-rocks, and has been developed over the past two decades delivering the giant Hibernian Field with about 700 Mb. It too is approaching maturity. A third province is the Mackenzie Delta and Arctic Islands which are predominantly gas prone. Hopes for new discovery off the Pacific Coast are likely to be

204

dashed as this does not seem to be a very prospective geological setting. (1)

It is again difficult to draw the boundary, but, as assessed here, the production of *Regular Conventional Oil* commenced in 1868 and grew at a low rate over the succeeding years to pass 170 kb/d in 1951. It then increased rapidly to a peak in 1973 of 1.7 kb/d before declining to 0.9 Mb/d in 2010. It is now set to decline at an indicated Depletion Rate of 5.2% a year. Canada consumes some 806 Mb/a year of which it has to import 62%.

Gas production has been increasing progressively since the early years of the last century to reach a plateau at about 6 Tcf a year. The resource is now 80% depleted, meaning that production is likely to decline at the present Depletion Rate of around 15% a year. (2)

(^{1})C.J. Campbell: Campbell's Atlas of Oil and Gas Depletion. Colin J. Campbell and Alexander Wöstmann 2013. P 343: 344

(^{2})C.J. Campbell: Campbell's Atlas of Oil and Gas Depletion. Colin J. Campbell and Alexander Wöstmann 2013. P 344

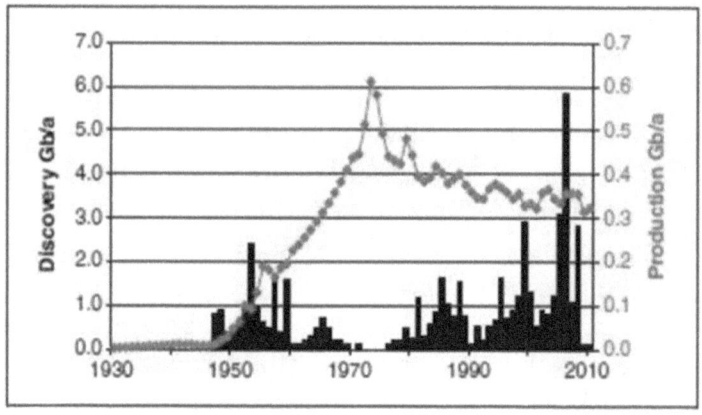

Canada discovery and production

Before the approval of the Kyoto Protocol in 1997, Canada was among the countries most active in the negotiations which led to the signing of the important agreement. It is somewhat surprising that Canada is the only country to 'repudiate' it (in 2012). In fact, the protocol did not have an easy life from the start and it took several years to enter into force because some countries were slow to ratify it and some, like the U.S., never ratified it. Nevertheless, the Canadian repudiation is unique. Understanding the reasons why this country arrived at its drastic decision is outside the scope of this study, but it gives an indication of the chances of such an agreement, which is needed to mitigate the global climate bad, being enforced, or if instead there is no way of expecting countries to cooperate for the provision of a global public good.

Canada is an interesting case study: it is a rich developed country, a democracy with a well-educated population on average. Its educational system relies on science as in other western economies and Canada enjoys a good reputation among the club of developed countries and so how it arrived at the repudiation is hard to say (as well as being beyond our scope), but two features emerge. First, it soon became clear that Canada was not on track with respect to the binding target of reducing emissions by 6 % by 2012 with respect to the base year 1990. Second, complaints were raised almost immediately about the little flexibility the agreement allowed.

Consequently, the standard argument (in addition to the one that big emitters such as China and India were not included) began to circulate: investments to enhance energy efficiency, a low-carbon energy infrastructure and new technologies would be the only way of making the energy system more environmentally sustainable.

Obviously, politics is the most significant explanatory variable and the change of Canadian government cannot be ignored, but no politicians actually denied the scientific basis of climate change and the responsibility of human activity. They simply wanted, or so they asserted, to adopt different instruments—namely clean technologies—to reduce emissions. In fact, it is now evident that Canada never reduced its emissions. On the contrary, GHG emissions have increased both in total and per capita terms and the country performs particularly badly in any ranking of developed countries. [1]

Although both the official repudiation and the great leap in oil sand production have happened in the last two years, a brief look at the history of the development of the tar sand market will reveal the importance of the economics of the oil industry and the oil price trend in the repudiation decision. The possibility of extracting oil from bitumen already existed at the beginning of the 20th century when a patent was granted for a hot water separation process. In fact, the Sun Oil Company opened its first mine in 1967 (producing just 30,000 barrels per day, compared with the current production of 1.9 million barrels per day according to the UK Tar Sands Network), but world oil prices were low

[1] Rossella Bardazzi • Maria Grazia Pazienza Alberto Tonini: European Energy and Climate Security. Springer International Publishing Switzerland 2016. P 170

and falling and so the industry did not develop. A second mine, operated by Syncrude Consortium, only came into operation in 1978, which is after the 1973 energy crisis. This crisis, known as the first oil shock, sent a signal to the oil industry that the price could in fact increase, after being incredibly low and stable for many years. With the 1979 energy crisis oil prices peaked again but declined again during the 80s to such low levels that the oil industry seemed to be in retrenchment. At the end of the century, oil sands production started to take off, but total unit production costs were too high with respect to oil prices and they had to be subsidized. For several years, no other mines were opened and the third one, operated by Shell Canada, appeared only in 2003. In fact, 2003 was very important for the development of the bitumen industry because the price of oil started to increase, rising to the famous $145 per barrel in January 2008, to make the industry very profitable. In 2008, Canada was not only not on track with its commitment to reduce its emissions by 2012, but it was actually knowingly increasing them, given the great expansion of bitumen production.

Indeed, the greenhouse gas emission intensity of bitumen and synthetic crude oil production is three times that of conventional oil. In fact, in 2012 Canadian oil sand production of crude bitumen and synthetic crude oil had increased by 30 % with respect to 2002, with the related emissions consequences thanks to hydraulic fracking technology. Despite differences in data estimation, all the sources that have estimated emissions show that oil sands are much greater GHG emitters than conventional oil processes (from a minimum of 5 % more up to 20 or 22 %—see footnote 13). The facts show, therefore, that Canada pursued the opposite of its commitment (i.e. emissions reduction). [1]

The earliest oil sands development started after World War I, when Canadian government surveyor, Sidney Ells, mapped the richest Sands deposits, and Karl Clark of the University of Alberta worked on extracting 100 percent clean bitumen and building the first pilot plants.

The need for oil and asphalt exploded in the twenties, as the automobile came of age and the Sands soon lured in various wealth seekers, including a group of New York City policemen who were convinced the Athabasca forest hid an enormous oil field. They lost their shirts. The North West Company Ltd., an

---

[1] Rossella Bardazzi • Maria Grazia Pazienza Alberto Tonini: European Energy and Climate Security. Springer International Publishing Switzerland 2016. P 171

Imperial Oil subsidiary, drilled a few wells in the Sands and found nothing. A Prince Edward Island promoter named Robert Fitzsimmons set up a small bitumen plant and sold barrels of the stuff to hardware stores as roof tar.

The first serious investor in the Sands was an enigmatic American geologist named Max Ball, who had advised Shell, Esso, and the White House, and was author of a lively bestseller called *This Fascinating Oil Business*. With some partners from Toronto, he built a small plant that actually produced diesel fuel and gasoline. The Canadian government took it over as a wartime reserve to supply U.S. troops in Alaska. Interest lagged after World War II, but with U.S. reserves starting to decline and "peak oil" worries rising, it took a Philadelphia oilman named J. Howard Pew, head of the Sun Oil Company, to make the final leap to large-scale production. His Great Canadian Oil Sands (GCOS) mine, which opened on September 30, 1967, burned through over $250 million before it started making a profit. Today run by Suncor Energy, the GCOS was the world's first complex dedicated to mining oil sands and upgrading bitumen into synthetic crude oil. [1]

---

[1] Alastair Sweeny: Black Bonanza. John Wiley & Sons Canada, Ltd. 2010. P 8:9

During his fifteen years developing a workable Sands project, Max Ball and his partners had funneled at least $700,000 into their oil sands lease, with the remainder —about $2 million—financed by Ottawa during the wartime emergency. To console themselves for their losses, Ball and his investors did retain a 25 percent interest in certain Athabasca properties, including a 4,000-acre lease beside Tar Island where Great Canadian Oil Sands would develop its first oil sands plant. [1]

Unfortunately for oil sands development, Imperial Oil's Leduc discovery in 1947 ensured that the development of the Athabasca Sands was no longer on the energy radar. Leduc, just south of Edmonton, was a huge conventional light crude oil reservoir, and other large discoveries followed close behind. The oil industry quickly lobbied Alberta to get out of direct investment in the oil sands business, and in 1955, the ARC unloaded the whole Bitumount operation for $180,000 to an entrepreneur named Stan Paulson. Paulson's CanAmera Oil Sands Development Ltd. confidently installed new Coulson separators based on spin-dry washers. Unfortunately, the abrasive quartz of the sands chewed up the separators in no time flat. Paulson unloaded the

---

[1] Alastair Sweeny: Black Bonanza. John Wiley & Sons Canada, Ltd. 2010. P 80

operation to the Imperial's Royalite Oil Company for $180,000 plus royalties. Royalite, in turn, was taken over by Gulf Oil and eventually became the property of Suncor Energy. [1]

Canada's oil sands are now the major whipping boy of European and American green groups fighting the "Great Climate War." Canada is an easy target. It's a breeze to beat up on America's little brother and the world's boy scout. [2]

7.7. Oil and gas production in USA

The key elements of this large diverse region are summarized here, excluding the deep water and Polar regions of Alaska, which do not qualify as *Regular Conventional Oil and Gas* by definition.

Prior to the opening of the Atlantic, some 200 million years ago, North America formed the western part of the Continent of Laurasia. The ancient Appalachian chain and

---

[1] Alastair Sweeny: Black Bonanza. John Wiley & Sons Canada, Ltd. 2010. P 83
[2] Alastair Sweeny: Black Bonanza. John Wiley & Sons Canada, Ltd. 2010. P 160

much of the interior is built of Palaeozoic rocks, laid down in geosynclinal troughs, being locally intruded by volcanic rocks, and deformed in mountain building movements in late Silurian and Permian times. [1]

The United States dominated world oil production in earlier years, being also the home to several of the world's major international oil companies. In 1930, it supplied about 65% of the World's production, but its share has since slipped to 21% in 1970 to less than 1% to-day. With its burgeoning domestic demand for oil, the country had become a net importer by 1950. Imports began to rise rapidly after peak production in 1970, such that they have now passed 70%.

The irreversible decline of its production means that even if demand were to be held static, the country would be importing 90% of its needs by 2020. It explains why access to foreign oil has long been officially declared a vital national interest, prompting military intervention.

---

[1]C.J. Campbell: Campbell's Atlas of Oil and Gas Depletion. Colin J. Campbell and Alexander Wöstmann 2013. P 347: 348

Different databases give different values but based on that provided by the Energy Information Agency it is assessed here that production of *Regular Conventional* oil commenced in 1859, passing 100 kb/d by 1890. It then rose to an overall peak of 9.4 Mb/d in 1970. It has since declined to 4.2 Mb/d and is set to continue to decline at about 5% a year.

Gas production commenced in the 1930s as a market developed for it. It depletes differently from oil; its production being generally capped below capacity by the pipeline infrastructure. The resulting plateau of production is now coming to an end, giving rise to high prices, prompting a new drilling boom. But the new wells have had to be produced at maximum rate and, as a result, are depleted within a matter of months. Some extra late-stage gas is being obtained by the tapping of the gas caps of oil fields during their dying days.

Gas production increased from 21 Tcf in 1990 to almost 23 Tcf in 2010, some 84% of the total endowment has now been produced, such that the production is likely to fall steeply at about 10% a year. The production of natural gas liquids, now running at about 1.9 Mb/d, will fall in parallel with the gas. There are, in addition, large amounts of nonconventional gas in the form of coal-bed methane, and in the so-called tight reservoirs, contributing about 10% of total supply. Electricity demand is growing, with many gas- fired generators under construction. As a result, the United States will have an increasingly desperate need to tap Arctic gas, possibly draining Canada in the process. [1]

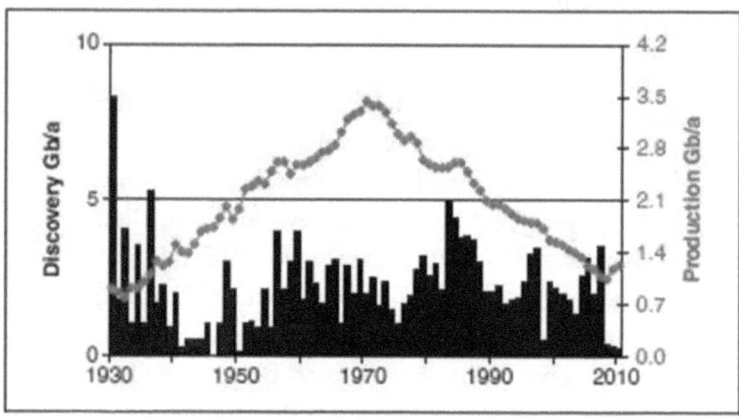

USA discovery and production

U.S. oil production may reach an all-time high of 10 million bpd before the end of this year, according to Rystad Energy. The energy data warehouse said its analysis shows production growing by an average 95,000 bpd each month of 2017. All of the growth stems

---

[1]C.J. Campbell: Campbell's Atlas of Oil and Gas Depletion. Colin J. Campbell and Alexander Wöstmann 2013. P 348: 349

from shale drilling, as the more modest growth from Deepwater Gulf of Mexico production is offsetting declines from other conventional oilfields.

The historic record of 10 million bpd was reached during November 1970 when U.S. oil prices were around $3 per barrel. This record was nearly broken in April 2015, when production reached 9.6 million barrels, before dropping 1 million bpd for 18 months as oil prices fell.

"U.S. oil production has grown faster at $50 than any analysts in the market predicted," said Bjornar Tonhaugen, vice president Oil Markets at Rystad Energy. "As these numbers are getting confirmed, the initial optimism about OPEC's temporary cuts, may turn to increasing skepticism about OPEC's choice of policy once the current output deal expires next year." [1]

Many factors interplayed to make the shale revolution a concrete reality in the US: the geological, institutional and market conditions were favorable to this drastic transformation. First of all, oil and gas quotations had remained

[1] U.S. oil production may reach record high in 2017 Gulf Publishing Co. 2017

high for sufficiently long to make investments in hydraulic fracturing profitable, and dynamic medium-sized energy companies took advantage of easy credit conditions to finance their exploration and exploitation projects. Furthermore, the US territories rich in shale reserves are generally scarcely populated and according to US law landowners also own the right to subsoil exploitation. This allows companies to sign contracts with private citizens, overcoming the normative and political obstacles which usually occur when subsoil exploitation is subject to public licensing. Finally, environmental laws, less strict than in other regions of the world, were essentially suspended for hydrofracking when this technique started to proliferate.

After a decade of stagnation, domestic natural gas production grew by a quarter between 2007 and 2013 thanks to SG, exceeding the US 1973 peak by more than 10 %. In 2013, the supply of SG was eight times the volume extracted in 2007 and represented almost 45 % of the overall US natural gas supply.

Similarly, as the production of LTO boomed, the crude oil supply resumed, reversing the negative trend prevailing since the mid-eighties with LTO reaching 3.5 million barrels per day (Mb/d) in 2013, out of the total of 7.7

Mb/d of crude produced by the US. The repercussions of the SF surge in the international energy markets have been dramatic: between 2007 and 2013 around two thirds of the increase in the world supply of both oil and natural gas came from SFs. In 2013 SG represented almost 9 % of the global supply and LTO a non-negligible 4 %. The effects on the US economy were also striking: [1]

1. In 2013 the US extracted 21 % of world natural gas and 11.5 % of oil, becoming the largest gas producer in 2009 and the principal oil supplier in 2012.

2. Its dependence on energy imports shrank: in 2013 the share of net imports in energy consumption fell to 19 from 30 % in 2005. As the volume of oil products and natural gas exports has doubled over the last five years, the energy component of the 2013 trade deficit was more than half compared to 2011.

3. US energy prices have remained well below the quotations prevailing in the rest of the world and this has boosted industrial competitiveness, especially of energy intensive industries. Lower

[1] Rossella Bardazzi • Maria Grazia Pazienza Alberto Tonini: European Energy and Climate Security. Springer International Publishing Switzerland 2016. P 134: 136

energy costs have encouraged additional foreign capital to flow into the US, adding to the ample fiscal advantage already existing for energy products, especially in comparison with European countries.

4. Looking forward, the substitution of coal with gas in the production of electricity may reduce air pollution via lower gas emissions. According to the US Energy Information Administration (EIA), in 2013 39 % of electricity was generated from coal and 27 % from natural gas (in 2008 these shares were 48 and 21 % respectively).

In the High Oil Price and High Oil and Gas Resource cases, growth in tight oil production results in significantly higher levels of total U.S. crude oil production than in the Reference case. Crude oil production in the High Oil and Gas Resource case increases to 16.6 million barrels per day (bbl/d) in 2040, compared with a peak of 10.6 million bbl/d in 2020 in the Reference case. In the High Oil Price case, production reaches a high of 13.0 million bbl/d in 2026, then declines to 9.9 million bbl/d in 2040 as a result of earlier resource development. In the Low Oil Price case, U.S. crude oil production totals 7.1 million bbl/d in 2040. The United States becomes a net petroleum exporter in 2021 in both the High Oil Price and High Oil and Gas Resource cases.

With lower levels of domestic production and higher domestic consumption in the Low Oil Price case, the net import share of total liquid fuels supply increases to 36% of total domestic supply in 2040. [1]

In the High Oil Price case, with higher world oil prices resulting in higher international natural gas prices, U.S. LNG exports climb to 8.1 Tcf in 2033 and account for 73% of total U.S. natural gas exports in 2040. In the High Oil and Gas Resource case, abundant U.S. dry natural gas production keeps domestic natural gas prices lower than international prices, supporting the growth of U.S. LNG exports, which total 10.3 Tcf in 2037 and account for 66% of total U.S. natural gas exports in 2040. In the Low Oil Price case with lower world oil prices, U.S. LNG exports are less competitive and grow more slowly, to a peak of 0.8 Tcf in 2018, and account for 13% of total U.S. natural gas exports in 2040. [2]

The discovery that seepages of "rock oil" flowing from below the ground could unveil astonishing reservoirs of petroleum prompted a rush for deep drilling in Pennsylvania, the

[1] U.S. Energy Information Administration. Annual Energy Outlook 2015. P 12
[2] U.S. Energy Information Administration. Annual Energy Outlook 2015. P 12: 13

United States and, later in Azerbaijan, Russia. From 1859 and 1870 onward, the contemporary oil industry began to take hold and the market swiftly organized the downstream areas of transport, storage, packing, refining and distribution. One of the most distinctive traits of this "build and grow" phase was the existence of a dual economy in the markets for products obtained by refining:

While some products came to the fore as global goods, e.g., kerosene for illumination and lubricating oils for greasing machines that were soon integrated in worldwide distribution networks, the remaining by-products (naphtha, gas oil, fuel oil, paraffin) lagged behind as regional-tradable goods which meant they could only be sold near their production source. From a technical standpoint, the bulk of these poorly tradable by-products came from the "bottom fraction" of crude oil—the last fractions with heavier molecules removed from the stills or leftover as residuum.

In the late nineteenth century, all distillation—the heart of refining operations—was performed in "straight-run" stills by gradually raising the temperature so as to drive vapor from the boiling oil along a pipe. Once in the pipe, the steam was normally condensed to a liquid by means of a condenser box with many pipes containing running water. When the specific gravity of the distillate reached a certain level, thus becoming too heavy, it was separated or "cut" by running the distillate into another tank. Due to the application of more intensive heat, the next component of the crude was then removed by means of steam and cooling devices again.

Since each successive still with its higher temperature was placed below the preceding one, gravity allowed the oil to flow steadily through the entire batch. The technical jargon— "batch-operation" captures precisely the system's basic feature.

In the end, the different fractions were separated by boiling edges ranging from the lighter by-products of naphtha and kerosene to the medium boiling range of gas oil, and to the "bottom" of heavier distillates: paraffin wax, lubricating oil, and fuel oil. The "batch-still" process was accompanied by other methods that consisted of simply skimming or topping, i.e., distillation of the naphtha and kerosene with steam and fire followed by the extraction of the fuel oil.

Significantly, most of the technological improvements that appeared in the

United States sought to improve the separation of the different "cuts" and, whenever possible, to convert the fractions of little market values to those of greater appeal. At a time when the demand for private lighting was reaching extraordinary heights, the kerosene "fraction" naturally became the most valued product and the mainstay of the oil economy. Moreover, its use in lamps had a profound effect on everyday life from Europe to the Pacific. The efficiency of kerosene was similar in candle-hours per unit of energy input to the existing alternatives of "portable" light–tallow candles, colza oil, and whale oil, but it was cleaner, burned without unpleasant smells, required only half the storage space, and, above all, was much cheaper. Estimates of the prices of the light flux (dollars per lumen hours) with the available technology of nineteenth-century lamps revealed that kerosene was 14–20 times cheaper than other substitutes of vegetable and animal oils. On the basis of the high demand for this new substitute good, some of the first contemporary multinational corporations soon concentrated trade along five major routes: North America to Western Europe; North America to South America and the Pacific; Rumania and Poland (Galicia) to Central and Western Europe; Dutch East Indies to East Asia; and Burma to South Asia. As the integration process and competition in these markets began to take hold, the sales of the other by-products from crude oil receded to the backstage as regional-tradable, or even non-marketable goods: In the USA, some fractions below the boiling range of kerosene, e.g., the volatile naphtha fraction, were generally thrown away with ecological impacts on lands and lakes; at best, the heavier fractions of gas oil and fuel oil were used by the oil enterprises for their own consumption in boilers and, at worst, "run into lakes of liquid petroleum which were set on fire to get rid of them" or alternatively "carried by pipes into the sea. Whatever the case, fuel oil had little or no market value.

There are two explanations for why oil was wasted in this manner: First the light density of the Pennsylvania crude made it suitable for refining into illuminants allowing yields of 65–75 % of kerosene until security and technical regulations were set. The potential for developing economies of scale for others by-products was substantially reduced as only small amounts of residuum were left over. Secondly, petroleum was discovered in the vicinity of major coal producing centers, thus hampering its acceptance as a substitute fuel. Overall, the shortcomings that affected the bottom fractions of oil enabled the reinforcement of a highly competitive and globalized sector based on the "upper" fractions of illuminants. [1]

[1] Nuno Luis Madureira: Key Concepts in Energy. Springer International Publishing Switzerland 2014. P 55: 57

The year 1956 was a significant one in petroleum history. In September 1956, at a meeting of the American Petroleum Institute in San Antonio, Texas, Shell's head geologist M. King Hubbert made the precise and shocking prediction that U.S. conventional oil output was going to peak in the early 1970s and, thereafter, decline, making the U.S. increasingly dependent on foreign suppliers. This was such bad news for the industry that Shell's public relations department made a desperate attempt to stop the speech and failed.

The founding father of the peak oil theory was the first to grasp the mechanics of oilfield depletion and the first to accurately assess recoverable oil reserves. Hubbert was right on the money about America, formerly the world's number one oil exporter. By 1970, production of petroleum (crude oil and natural gas plant liquids) in the lower forty-eight U.S. states would reach its highest level, peaking at 9.4 million barrels per day. North Slope discoveries in Alaska gave the U.S. a couple of years of grace, but output steadily declined ever afterward, and from that time forward, the U.S. grew more and more dependent on foreign oil. [1]

---

[1]Alastair Sweeny: Black Bonanza. John Wiley & Sons Canada, Ltd. 2010. P 95

7.8. Oil and gas Production in UK

the UK has had two oil production peaks, with the trough between these being caused mainly by safety work carried out on all fields following the Piper-Alpha disaster in 1988. Lesser factors for this production trough include the 2-year work-over on Brent due to high gas production; the fall in oil prices post-1984; anticipated changes in petroleum revenue tax that may have delayed the start-up of new fields; and—as Laherrère notes—the secondary peak in discovery in the late 1980s, as indicated in Fig. Without this 'trough', production most likely would have risen to a peak in the early 1990s. As it was, the UK's conventional oil resource-limited peak occurred in 1999, at 59 % of Campbell's estimate of URR.

To compare to the simple model of Figs. gives the corresponding plot of UK production broken down by field.

As the Figure shows, except for the 'trough', this plot of a region of mainly offshore fields is more like the simple model of Fig. than the corresponding plot for Germany, which is primarily of onshore fields. This is not surprising, as the simple model was originally devised from examination of UK data.

227

Although discovery is not broken out by field in Fig. the pattern of UK discovery roughly matches that of the Fig. once a small initial field had been discovered in 1969, nearly all the very large fields were discovered fairly rapidly thereafter. As can be seen, the explanation is supported that peak is caused by a

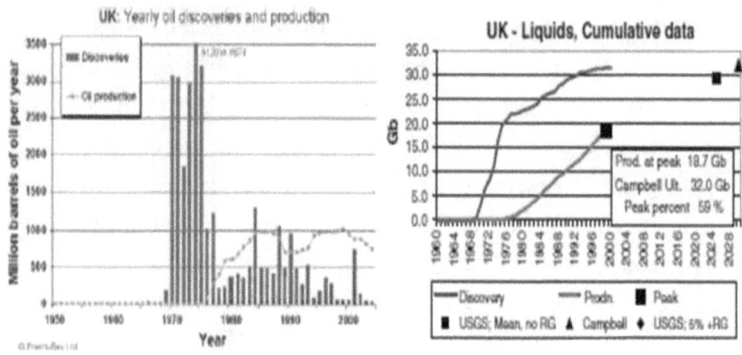

region's large fields mostly getting into production first and then declining. In addition, by comparing the volume discovered with the volume produced, and using the 'peak at mid-point' rule, it was clear that the 1984 peak was not resource-limited, while the 1999 peak would appear to be.

But now we have to return to the important question raised above for Germany.

How are we sure that the UK's 1999 peak was indeed resource-limited? This is clearly the case if based on the oil already discovered by that date; but how do we know that the UK does not have has big new plays of conventional oil waiting in the wings that will yield enough oil to surpass the 1999 peak? As already mentioned, this situation can occur where the historical discovery data (the 'creaming curve' vs. time) indicates an apparent asymptote, but where this asymptote increases as a major new play enters the scene.

The answer, as already mentioned in connection with Germany, is that knowledge of peak cannot be based solely on discovery data, it must also include geological appraisal. It is recognized that the latter will always be judgement, and that the chance of future large finds cannot be known with certainty. But a great deal of geological knowledge now exists for much of the world's likely oil plays, and as explained later, globally the discovery of conventional oil in new fields has been

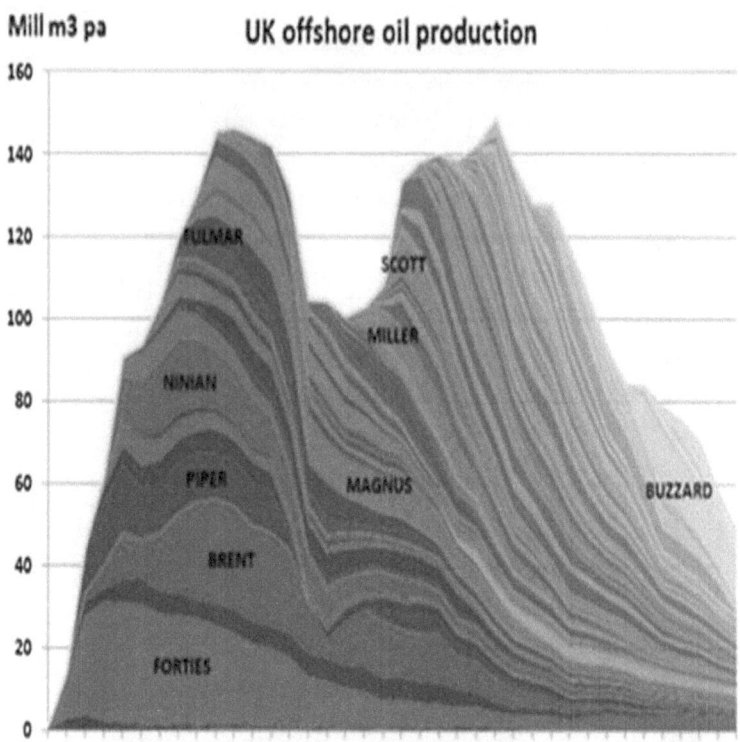

Source of data: https://www.og.decc.gov.uk/pprs/full_production.htm

http://crudeoilpeak.info/uk-peak

falling for about half a century, so the scope for surprises in terms of big new discoveries is now judged generally as rather small.

Note however that in the UK's case, as elsewhere, even for conventional oil there are still significant future potential sources of oil. Some experts suggest that there remain quite large quantities of UK oil undiscovered in subtle stratigraphic traps; there is certainly still potential in the deeper Atlantic; and there is known to be a large amount of oil currently in-place in existing fields deemed unrecoverable with today's technology and oil price.

But geological and reservoir knowledge says it is virtually certain that none of this UK oil, where it exists, can be developed rapidly enough to push production back up past the 1999 peak. The subtle traps, if they hold significant amounts of oil, will need highly calibrated seismic to find, so will not be found rapidly; the deeper Atlantic will offer surprises but is not thought especially prospective due to poor source rock and traps; while the many routes to improved recovery (EOR) in existing fields have already seen much trial and analysis. Overall, combining the UK's discovery data with geological knowledge indicates that the country's conventional oil peak in 1999 was indeed resource-limited.

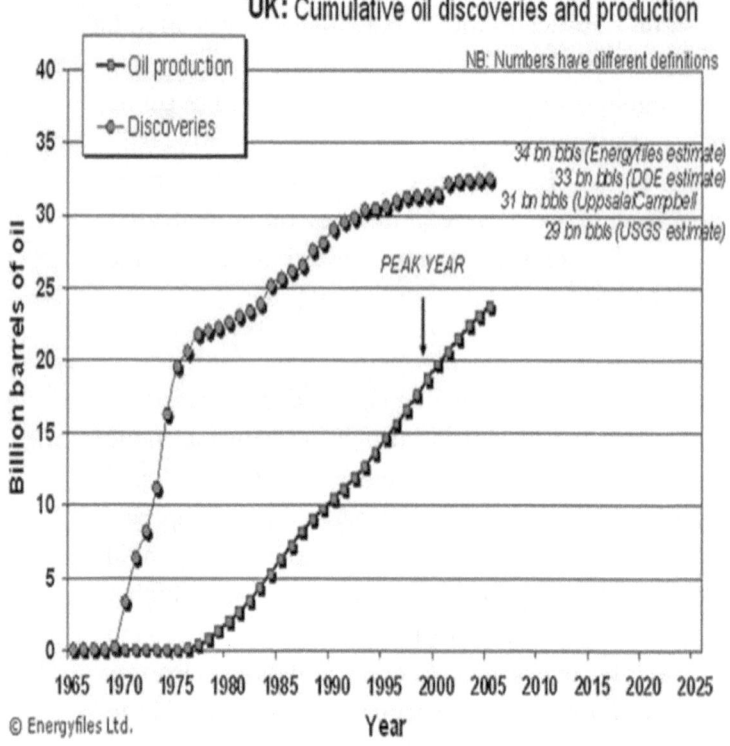

The Figure brought out this point by giving two estimates of the UK's ultimately recoverable conventional oil resource (URR); that of the USGS Assessment of year-2000; mean value and without allowance for reserves growth, and Campbell's of about the same date, both ex-NGLs. As with the case of Germany, these estimates are close to each other, and also broadly in agreement with the value that might be expected from extrapolating by eye the backdated industry discovery data. Three further estimates of the UK's conventional oil URR are given in Fig. The earliest is a UK government DoE 'Brown Book' estimate made back in 1974 (see Annex 2); and the more recent are those from University of Uppsala/Campbell and Energy Files Ltd, both made around 2004. As the Figure shows, these 'ultimate' are again in close agreement with each other, and with the asymptote of the discovery creaming curve.

Given that nearly all of the UK's large fields, and over half of the UK's total oil, had been discovered by the time offshore production started in 1975, it is not surprising that realistic estimates of the UK's conventional oil ultimate were available from an early date. These included the UK Department of Energy's 1974 estimate of 4500 million tons (33 Gb) shown in Fig.

Then using the 'mid-point' rule—well known and well understood at the time— it was easy to predict that UK production would peak at, or probably a bit before, the point where about half of this (i.e., 16.5 Gb) had been produced. Looking at Fig. this meant around the mid-1990s if the slowdown due to the 'production trough' is ignored. It was this understanding of the likely date of peak—well known within the industry—that allowed a 1976 UK research study for the government to note that the date of the world oil peak (at "about [the year] 2000") would not be far behind that of the UK peak.

However, somehow this information on the UK peak got lost. In about 1997 and 1998 our small ad hoc Oil Research Group at the University of Reading tried several times to warn the UK's Dept. of Trade and Industry (DTI) of the coming global peak of conventional oil production, where our line of argument was simple: 'You understand the mechanism behind the coming UK peak, and you know that this is close; the world peak works in rather the same way, and the discovery data show that is fairly close also'.

Unfortunately, this argument fell completely flat. The concept of 'mid-point peak' had been forgotten (and not just in the UK), and a deep myth had developed instead based on the evolution of proved reserves. In the UK, for example, UK proved reserves had held steady since about 1980 at between 4 and 5 Gb, despite annual production being nearly 1 Gb/y for most of this period (Annex 2). As a result, this nearly two decades of there apparently being only roughly '5 years' supply' of UK oil remaining (plus corresponding data for other countries) had fooled nearly all analysts (including many within the oil industry, and most within the UK government and also at the IEA) into thinking that this 'replacement of reserves' was primarily due to improvements in technology; with horizontal drilling and 4-D seismic being widely cited. Our arguments about the proximity of the global oil peak were therefore seen as baseless because the DTI were convinced that the UK peak itself was still many years away; and that afterwards production would decline only gradually anyway, because of future gains in technology. (For a fuller discussion of these meetings with the UK's DTI and with other government bodies.

Nevertheless, despite the DTI's skepticism, the UK peak was indeed close.

Today we can give the UK as an example of a country where, for conventional oil, only modest scope remains for new discoveries, where the likely total recoverable quantity of this oil is judged well over half depleted, and where the country's resource-limited oil production peak of this oil is past. [1]

---

[1] R.W. Bentley: Introduction to Peak Oil. Springer International Publishing Switzerland 2016. P 26: 31

References

1. Alastair Sweeny: Black Bonanza. John Wiley & Sons Canada, Ltd. 2010.
2. Ali Nezihi Bilge • Ayhan Özgür Toy Mehmet Erdem Günay: Energy Systems and Management. Springer International Publishing Switzerland 2015.
3. C.J. Campbell: Campbell's Atlas of Oil and Gas Depletion. Colin J. Campbell and Alexander Wöstmann 2013.
4. Cyrus Bina: A Prelude to the Foundation of Political Economy. PALGRAVE MACMILLAN. 2013.
5. Dr.Mansour Soliman: NATURAL GAS: INVESTMENT STRATEGIES IN AN UNCERTAIN WORLD.
6. Frank Jahn, Mark Cook and Mark Graham: HYDROCARBON EXPLORATION AND PRODUCTION. 2ND EDITION. Elsevier B.V. 2008.
7. Georgios M. Kopanos · Pei Liu Michael C. Georgiadis: Advances in Energy Systems Engineering. Springer International Publishing Switzerland 2017.
8. Hengyun Ma 1 Les Oxley: China's Energy Economy. Springer-Verlag Berlin Heidelberg 2012.
9. Henrik Wachtmeister, Linnea Lund, Kjell Aleklett, and Mikael Hook. Production Decline Curves of Tight Oil Wells in Eagle Ford Shale. Natural Resources Research. 2017.

10. Iakovos Alhadeff: USA Russia & China in the Middle East. Free ebook.net 2014.
11. Irwin A. Wiehe: Process Chemistry of Petroleum Macromolecules. Taylor & Francis Group, LLC. 2008.
12. J. Edward Gates • David L. Trauger • Brian Czech: Peak Oil, Economic Growth, and Wildlife Conservation. Springer Science+Business Media New York 2014.
13. James G. Speight: The Chemistry and Technology of Petroleum. FOURTH EDITION. Taylor & Francis Group, LLC. 2007.
14. Jinjun Xue • Zhongxiu Zhao • Yande Dai • Bo Wang: Green Low-Carbon Development in China. Springer International Publishing Switzerland 2013.
15. Joseph Tawonezvi: The legal and regulatory framework for the EU' shale gas exploration and production regulating public health and environmental impacts. Energ. Ecol. Environ. 2017.
16. K E N N E T H S . D E F F E Y E S: Hubbert's Peak. Princeton University Press. 2001.
17. Kirsten Heimann • Obulisamy Parthiba Karthikeyan Subramanian Senthilkannan Muthu: Biodegradation and Bioconversion of Hydrocarbons. Springer Science+Business Media Singapore 2017.
18. Leo Lester: Energy Relations and Policy Making in Asia. 2016.

19. Marawan , H.: Maximization of Egyptian Gas Oil Production Through the Optimal Use of the Operating Parameters.
20. Mario Alberto Hernández Nilda González • Lisandro Hernández: Hydrogeology of a Large Oil-and-Gas Basin in Central Patagonia. 2017.
21. Marja Jarvela • Sirkku Juhola: Energy, Policy, and the Environment. Springer Science+Business Media, LLC 2011.
22. Michael Ala: The Imperial College Lectures in PETROLEUM ENGINEERING. World Scientific Publishing Europe Ltd. 2017.
23. Michael D. Max · Arthur H. Johnson William P. Dillon: Natural Gas Hydrate – Arctic Ocean Deepwater Resource Potential. 2013.
24. Nnaemeka Vincent Emodi: Energy Policies for Sustainable Development Strategies. Springer Science+Business Media Singapore 2016.
25. Nuno Luis Madureira: Key Concepts in Energy. Springer International Publishing Switzerland 2014.
26. Organization of the Petroleum Exporting Countries. Annual Report 2014.
27. Patrick A. Narbel • Jan Petter Hansen Jan R. Lien: Energy Technologies and Economics. Springer International Publishing Switzerland 2014.
28. R.W. Bentley: Introduction to Peak Oil. Springer International Publishing Switzerland 2016.
29. Ripudaman Malhotra: Fossil Energy. Springer Science+Business Media New York 2013.

30. Roger Boyd: Energy and the Financial System Springer Cham Heidelberg New York Dordrecht London 2013.
31. Rossella Bardazzi • Maria Grazia Pazienza Alberto Tonini: European Energy and Climate Security. Springer International Publishing Switzerland 2016.
32. Sidney Borowitz: FAREWELL FOSSIL FUELS Reviewing America' s. Energy Policy. Plenum Press, New York in 1999.
33. Simone Tagliapietra: Energy Relations in the Euro-Mediterranean. 2017.
34. Thijs Van de Graaf • Benjamin K. Sovacool Arunabha Ghosh • Florian Kern • Michael T. Klare: The Palgrave Handbook of the International Political Economy of Energy. 2016.
35. U.S. Energy Information Administration. Annual Energy Outlook 2015.
36. **U.S. oil production may reach record high in 2017 Gulf Publishing Co. 2017**
37. Uttam Ray Chaudhuri: Fundamentals of Petroleum and Petrochemical Engineering. Taylor and Francis Group. 2011.
38. w. T. Ziemba S. L. Schwartz: ENERGY POLICY MODELING: UNITED STATES AND CANADIAN EXPERIENCES Volume II. Martinus Nijhoff Publishing, Boston 1st edition 1980.
39. Walter Leal Filho • Vlasios Voudouris: Global Energy Policy and Security. Springer-Verlag London 2013.

40. Yi-Ming Wei • Hua Liao: Energy Economics: Energy Efficiency in China. Springer International Publishing Switzerland 2016.

Biography of the author

Roshdy Ebrahim Abdin, Egyptian.

Ph.D (economics)

Economic lecturer.

Member at the Egyptian assembly for political economy.

Member at the Egyptian assembly for international law.

Professional diploma in arbitration.

diploma in importing and exporting.

Lawyer since 2008.

For more information please subscribe to my blog:

http://roshdyebrahim.blogspot.com.eg/

the author's books
1. Economic study of Oil and Gas Well Drilling
2. Economic study of Oil and Gas Exploration
3. Economics of oil petroleum, principles
4. Economics of Petroleum reservoirs
5. Economics of petroleum market
6. Explanatory of petroleum market volatility

www.ingramcontent.com/pod-product-compliance
Lightning Source LLC
Chambersburg PA
CBHW031616210526
45464CB00004B/1602